Britain's Strangest True Crime Cases

Dylan Frost

Contents

INTRODUCTION

The history of true crime in Britain is a long and, as we shall see, often stranger than fiction tale. The book that follows offers an eclectic stew of strange and perplexing British true crime cases. These cases are all disconcertingly odd and in many instances downright bizarre. We have the case of an elderly farmer brutally murdered with a pitchfork. The police officers who investigated this case soon stumbled into whispers of witchcraft as a possible motive. Then there is a shocking train murder which took place in a closed carriage in broad daylight during an afternoon commuter run to London. We also have the baffling case of a retired spinster who was gruesomely killed for no apparent reason in her own home on Halloween night.

Rest assured, there's still plenty more to come. We shall also be examining the legend of the alleged maniac said to randomly push his victims into Manchester's murky canals.

Then we'll take a look at the Victorian terror known as Spring-Heeled Jack. We shall stop too to consider the unsolved murder of a young man in Sussex who was found dissected inside two abandoned suitcases. Could Reggie Kray have been responsible for this grisly murder? He was but one of several suspects. We shall also explore the high profile killing of Jill Dando - a case which surely ranks as one of the most shocking and most baffling celebrity deaths ever to occur in Britain.

As if that wasn't enough we also have grave robbers, cannibals, a woman who staged the hoax abduction of her own daughter, the Brighton trunk murders, a gruesome killer who operated at the same time as Jack the Ripper and had the macabre signature of leaving torsos and body parts scattered around London, and a suave post-war con artist who in reality was a depraved sexual serial killer. Hopefully I have done justice to these fascinatingly bizarre cases and there will plenty of details that even the most hardened true crime buff may not have been familiar with before.

As far as weird true crime in Britain goes, there are no shortage of bewildering and baffling cases. I hope to explore more of these cases in the future but for now I hope you enjoy this initial volume. So, draw the curtains, turn off the lights, make sure the doors are locked, and settle down to explore some of the strangest true crime cases Blighty has to offer...

WITCHCRAFT IN WARWICKSHIRE?
- THE STRANGE MURDER OF
CHARLES WALTON

On the 14th of February 1945, a 74 year-old farm worker named Charles Walton was found dead in a field called Hillground at Firs Farm on the slopes of Meon Hill, Lower Quinton in Warwickshire. Walton had been out cutting some hedges when he was murdered. He had arthritis and used a walking stick. Walton would not have been capable of putting up much of a fight so this murder seemed to be thoroughly wicked and perplexingly senseless at first glance. The fact that someone had murdered an elderly and harmless farm worker was baffling enough but the absolutely brutal and gruesome nature of the murder added even more mystery to the case. Something very strange and unfathomable had happened in that field and you could only feel sympathy for the poor police officers who had to somehow make any sense out of this this weird and shocking mystery.

Walton had been killed with his own pitchfork and billhook (a billhook or bill hook is a sharp tool used widely in agriculture and forestry for cutting woody material such as shrubs, small trees and branches). This was the sort of barbarous blood drenched murder that Jason Vorhees or Michael Myers would carry out in a schlocky horror movie. Why all the vicious violence against an old man who worked on a farm? It's not as if Walton would have put up much of a struggle when he was killed. And what exactly had Charles Walton done to deserve this anyway? Walton had been pinned to the floor by the pitchfork and his own farming hook was lodged in his throat.

Dr AR McWhinny, a local doctor, made the following notes on the horrendous injuries to the murdered Walton - 'The body was lying on its left side with the knees and hips in a bent position. There was a gash on the right side of the neck involving the main structures of the neck, and the cut ends of main vessels and the lacerated windpipe could be seen. The tip

of a billhook [was] buried at least four inches in the tissue at
the front of the neck. In addition the face was impaled by a
pitchfork, one prong entered on either side of the face just
below and in front of the angle of the jaw. The handle of the
fork had been pressed backwards and the end of the handle
was wedged under the cross member of the hedge behind the
head, thus anchoring the head to the ground.'

Walton had also been beaten with his own walking stick (that
DEFINITELY felt like overkill given that the poor man had
already been cut to ribbons with various farming implements!)
and had numerous bruises all over his body. His head was
nearly severed and he had some broken ribs. The killer had not
been content with merely murdering Charles Walton. He had
also battered and beaten the body with what you can only
describe as crazed and savage aggression and anger. The police
were now faced with an obvious question. Was the killer was a
random lunatic who had stumbled across Walton in that field
by accident or did he know Charles Walton? Was the murder
premeditated? If the latter was the case then what would be
the motive to kill a 74 year-old arthritic farm worker in such
bloodthirsty fashion?

Charles Walton had lived with his niece in a cottage on the
land owned by the farm. Though he was said to be a man who
kept himself to himself and didn't mix much (you wouldn't
really expect an elderly farm worker to be much of a man
about town), Walton was respected for his work ethic on the
farm and said to be liked by those who had any contact with
him. Well, not quite everyone. As we shall see, there were
those in the area who felt there was something of the night
about Charles Walton. On the surface though, Walton was
seemingly not the sort of man to have enemies or attract any
attention whatsoever. His murder was completely baffling.
One minute he was happily trimming some hedges and the
next minute he'd been attacked by a maniac with a pitchfork.

Charles Walton had been found by his niece Edith and a farm
worker named Harry Beasley. Walton had failed to come home

for his tea so Edith had got worried and enlisted Harry to
come out to the fields with her to look for her uncle -
whereupon they were eventually met with this most grisly and
shocking discovery. The ground around Walton was covered in
blood and it was a sight that poor Edith would never be able to
forget. One wouldn't be surprised if the gruesome image of her
dead uncle in that lonely field gave her nightmares for years to
come. It wasn't the sort of thing you expect to happen on a
quiet and peaceful farm. In fact, it wasn't the sort of thing you
expect to happen anywhere.

The Deputy Chief Constable of Warwickshire, understandably
perplexed by this strange murder, decided to ask Scotland
Yard for help in investigating the case. In no time at all the
murder of Charles Walton became a knotty mystery from
which various outlandish subplots began to spiral. One early
theory by the local police was that the murderer could have
been an Italian POW being held in the area. World War 2,
though in its final months in Europe (Italy had been knocked
out of the war and the Nazis were almost finished), was still
somehow rumbling on and large numbers of former Italian
soldiers were still held in Britain. The Allied forces had taken
hundreds of thousands of Italian prisoners in North Africa
alone when the Axis position there collapsed earlier in the war.

The Italian prisoners of war in Warwickshire had a surprising
amount of freedom and were apparently allowed to take walks
and even go to the cinema. They didn't really seem to be
prisoners at all in the traditional sense. Given that the Italians
could more or less come and go as they pleased, the police
decided that they had to at least probe the theory that one of
these Italians had wandered onto the farm and murdered
Charles Walton. The Italian POW theory seemed to be a blind
alley in the end though. Scotland Yard, through the use of
interpreters, questioned a large number of Italian POWs but
never arrested anyone. There was never any evidence which
linked any of the Axis POWs in the area to Walton's murder.
This obviously meant that the killer was much more likely to
be a local man (the brute force of the murder indicated that a

woman could not have done this) native to the area.

In contemporary accounts of this case it is sometimes reported that a cross had been carved into Walton's chest by the murderer. However, the police reports of the time make no blatant mention of this cross, or indeed any mention at all, so this detail must remain open to question. It could be that they kept this detail secret but no firm evidence for a bloodied carved cross on the dead body was ever verified or established as fact (as opposed to embellishment - much has doubtless been embellished in this case). Even without the grisly and sinister flourish of the cross carved into flesh though there was still plenty of strangeness about this murder. It was certainly not short of mystery or bewilderingly spooky trappings.

Detective Chief Inspector Robert Fabian, who was a pretty big cheese in police circles at the time, arrived in the area to investigate the case but soon found (much to his frustration you'd imagine) that the locals were strangely reluctant to talk to him about the murder of Charles Walton. They talked cryptically about bad crops and a ghostly black dog that was often seen on the land but they rather skirted around the central issue of Charles Walton being killed with a pitchfork. Fabian must have felt like he was in a folk horror movie like The Wicker Man at times as he tried to make sense of this bizarre murder. He was like that doctor who walks into the isolated rural pub in An American Werewolf in London - whereupon every goes quiet.

It was through what you might describe as occult research though that Fabian finally began to develop a few theories of his own that might potentially explain this mystery. These theories were outlandish and weird but that's where the evidence was leading Fabian so he had no choice but to accommodate these lines of inquiry - as bizarre as they might be or seem on the surface. Fabian began to read about the local folklore and learned that an ancient rural custom (if you can call it a custom) was that a witch must be killed by a pitchfork to banish the curse and ensure that the witch in question can't dispense any more evil.

As he pondered all of this occult folklore, Fabian began to seriously wonder if Walton had been killed in some weird ritualistic pagan murder. There were even veiled whispers that Walton had 'special' powers and dabbled in the occult. Was the murdered man the subject of local innuendo and legend which revolved around witchcraft and black magic? Was Charles Walton considered to be a wicca - a male witch? As for the evidence concerning an occult motive for this murder, Walton's garden was found to be festooned with natterjack toads and these toads have long been associated with witchcraft.

There were stories too that Walton could talk to animals and a mysterious pocket watch said to be symbolic of his connection to the occult was missing when he was found dead. The more that Fabian investigated this case the stranger it seemed to become. He wasn't quite sure what to make of what he had found so far but it was certainly all very bizarre. Perhaps the oddest discovery by Fabian was that a similar murder had occurred in Warwickshire 75 years before and about thirteen miles away from the spot where Walton was killed. All those years ago, a 79 year-old woman named Anne Tennant was murdered in Warwickshire by a farm worker with a pitchfork because he believed she was a witch.

The police at the time found that half the village where Tennant was killed believed in witchcraft. Fabian read of this murder in a book called Folklore, Old Customs and Superstitions in Shakespeare Land. Here was the REALLY spooky thing thing about the book though. It mentioned a local young plough boy who reported seeing ghosts on the land after Anne Tennant was killed. The name of the plough boy? Charles Walton. The book further claimed that a man named Charles Walton had died in 1885. This has led to theories that the Charles Walton in this 1945 murder case was a ghost!

It is believed that if people at the time suspected that a witch had put a curse on them the only way to banish the curse was to kill the witch. Fabian had to consider the possibility that something similar had happened in the case of Charles Walton. It was obviously all very outlandish though. Walton had apparently been very good at taming dogs and could get birds to flock to his hand to feed. He was an old country gentleman so none of these feats were what you would call supernatural or out of the ordinary. The locals though seemed to have taken Walton's skill with animals and somehow interpreted it as witchcraft.

Fabian begin to detect that some of the locals believed Walton had hexed the land and crops with his alleged dabblings in witchcraft. However outlandish this explanation might be it did at least provide one possible motive for why he might have been murdered. The area was dotted with ancient stones said to have once been the site of cult rituals and perhaps even sacrifices. Fabian heard many tales of mysterious spectral black dogs in the area and even alleged he saw one himself during his investigation. There was a local legend that the phantom hounds of the Celtic king Arawyn hunted the hill at night - which would explain why people in the area were so obsessed with sightings of strange dogs.

Margaret Murray, a professor from University College in London, believed that Walton's murder was a blood sacrifice designed to 'replenish' the soil. Walton was killed on Valentine's Day but this date also had an occult significance because it coincided with the Celtic Midwinter festival of Imbolc. Based on a Celtic tradition, Imbolc marks the halfway point between winter solstice and the spring equinox in Neolithic Ireland and Scotland. The holiday is celebrated by Wiccans and other practitioners of neopagan or pagan-influenced religions. When one tallies up all of this background detail it appears that this wasn't a simple case of murder at all. Such was the puzzle facing Fabian. He had the balance the witchcraft theory with more prosaic explanations in order to decipher what the real truth might be. That turned out to be a surprisingly complex and confusing task.

One other bizarre mystery in this case is the resting place of Charles Walton. He was buried in a churchyard near his cottage (his farm cottage actually still exists to this day) but his gravestone was then removed and no one now knows where exactly he is buried. Legend has it that locals moved the body and gravestone to banish any remaining curse he might bring upon the village. Walton is sometimes cited as the last 'witch killing' in England but his murder officially remains a mystery. Nothing was proven one way or the other. A more contemporary explanation for the burial mystery is that relatives of Walton decided to move his grave to a secret spot because they got fed up with people visiting the grave on the anniversary of his death. I'm not quite sure how you would label these visitors. True crime or witchcraft tourists perhaps?

Fabian certainly seemed open to the witchcraft theory and in his memoirs suggested that black magic and witchcraft should be approached with caution because we don't understand it and if you do venture in this mysterious realm you might meet a ghastly end like poor old Charles Walton. "I advise anybody who is tempted at any time to venture into Black Magic, witchcraft, Shamanism — call it what you will — to remember Charles Walton and to think of his death, which was clearly the ghastly climax of a pagan rite. There is no stronger argument for keeping as far away as possible from the villains with their swords, incense and mumbo-jumbo. It is prudence on which your future peace of mind and even your life could depend." It has been alleged that in 1960 the watch of Charles Walton was found and it turned out to be scrying glass. A scrying glass is a mirror that is used as a focal point for scrying or to encourage clairvoyance. Whether this coda is true or urban myth though, like so much of this case, remains open to question.

As for more prosaic explanations pertaining to this murder, one suspect was Edith's boyfriend Charles - although plainly there was insufficient evidence to ever charge him with anything. He was certainly someone the police would have investigated in thorough fashion though. The theory was that maybe Charles had murdered the old man to get his hands on the farm cottage and any inheritance. This theory though clearly had no legs and didn't stand up to much scrutiny. It is doubtful that Charles Walton would have had much money so what would be the point of killing him? Besides, he was 74 years-old and wasn't going to live forever anyway.

Perhaps the most interesting suspect in this murder is 40 year-old Alfred Potter. Potter lived on the farm (he managed The Firs for L. L. Potter & Co) and had known Walton for five years. He even employed Walton from time to time. The police were said to be rather suspicious of Potter and had him put under observation by a local constable. What made Potter suspicious to the police was that when they spoke to him several times there were discrepancies between his stories and accounts of his movements. They also found out that Potter would occasionally engage Walton's services for some farm work and then Walton would tell Potter how many hours he had worked in order to settle his wages.

The police had to consider the theory then that Walton had lied about working more hours than he did to extract more money from Potter and that maybe Potter had found about this and got angry about it. It was obviously a bit of a stretch to think that Potter had killed Walton with a pitchfork because of a dispute over a few shillings but it was at least a theory. Another factor was that Edith reported seeing Potter the day Walton was murdered. It was difficult to know though if this was significant or not. Potter was often seen on the farm so it could have been coincidence. He was close enough though to have potentially been involved in the murder.

The police found Potter to be very shaken and even shivering when Walton's body was found. He seemed to be in great distress but it's hard to say if this was guilt or just shock at learning of the brutal murder of someone he knew. Though his evidence was not terribly consistent and the police found him a rather sullen character (he was also someone of great strength and would have been physically capable of killing Walton) the police simply could not find sufficient evidence to prove that Potter had anything to do with the death. At one point the police noted that Potter (rather suspiciously) visited the scene of the murder but this could simply have been curiosity rather than a murderer taking a trip back to the scene of the crime.

There are stories that Potter owed Walton money (which would certainly supply a motive for the murder) but these rumours were later found to be incorrect. The police investigated Alfred Potter thoroughly and found no violent incidents in his past that might point to him being capable of murder. Nonetheless, Fabian, in his memoirs, said it was still perfectly possible that Potter might have killed Walton. In the end though they simply couldn't find any evidence to prove it so never went very far down this particular line of enquiry. The mystery of Charles Walton's death therefore retains plenty of secrets and seems destined to fascinate true crime buffs for many more decades - and perhaps even centuries - to come. If you do ever find yourself in the part of Warwickshire where Charles Walton was murdered keep a close eye out for any mysterious and ghostly black dogs. You never know when one might be following you.

DEATH LINE - THE CLOSED-CARRIAGE TRAIN MURDER MYSTERY

On the afternoon of Wednesday the 23rd of March 1988, 26 year-old Debbie Linsley boarded a fairly busy train at Petts Wood station at 2-16 in the afternoon. Debbie's destination was Victoria station in London. There were about nine stops between Petts Wood and Victoria and so Debbie had packed some sandwiches for the journey. There is nothing more hum-drum and ordinary than taking a train journey in the afternoon. You don't expect anything strange or disturbing to happen and it rarely does. This case would - tragically - turn out to be different though. Debbie Linsley was about to experience one of the most disturbing train rides in true crime history.

In those days the trains in Britain could still be pretty grim and dirty. The rail system in 1988 was in desperate need of investment and new rolling stock. If you hopped on a train in the 1980s you could be forgiven for thinking you were in a third world country or the Soviet Union. If we were to take a detour into politics for a moment one might argue that the Tory government deliberately underfunded the train system to make the case for privatisation. Anyone who remembers using trains in the 1980s will have memories of sitting on some dusty and dirty old seat in a clapped-out smelly train that should have been been put out to pasture years ago.

Believe it or not trains were so antiquated in those days that they didn't even have automatic doors. You had to open and close the door yourself - which was incredibly dangerous. Before the train left the station some poor train guard had to walk up and down the platform to make sure all the doors were properly shut. Another weird thing about trains in those days is that they had some closed carriages. That is to say that some of the carriages had no doors where you could move through the rest of the train.

If you sat in one of these closed carriages you were stuck in that single carriage until such time as you got out at a station. Closed carriages also meant that no member of staff could come into your carriage. That was great for fare dodgers but not so great for women travelling alone. Looking back closed carriages were obviously something with many potential dangers. What if a lone woman found herself in a closed carriage with a dangerous man? Tragically, this was the fate which befell Debbie Linsley.

Though she was safety conscious and apparently carried a 'rape whistle', Debbie had chosen to get on a closed carriage because she was a smoker and the closed-carriage on this train was a designated smoking carriage. Though she couldn't have known it at the time, choosing the closed carriage that afternoon would come at the cost of her life. There is a plausible theory that when Debbie got on the carriage there were some other passengers in there, including women - which made her feel safe. However, by the time of the attack people had got off at various stations leaving just Debbie and the assailant in the enclosed carriage.

Debbie Linsley was from Bromley in Kent but worked in Scotland's capital city in a hotel. She was back down south to complete a three day course on hotel management. Debbie's brother was due to get married in two weeks so Debbie was also looking for a bridesmaid's dress while she was home. More than anything Debbie was enjoying the fact that she could spend a few days with her family. Because she worked so far away it was rare for them all to be together like this.

Debbie's specific train journey that day was because she wanted look around the Sherlock Holmes Hotel in Baker Street. Debbie had been offered a job there by a man she met on her hotel management course and wanted to take a look at the place for herself before making a decision on whether to take up the position or not. Sadly though, Debbie would never make it to the Baker Street Hotel. Somewhere between Petts Wood station and Victoria something horrific and shocking had happened in that closed carriage. In the constricted and blocked space of the carriage no one had been able to help Debbie. In fact, only one person even reported hearing her scream.

When the train Debbie was on pulled into Victoria Station just before three in the afternoon a member of staff (who was checking the carriages for left luggage) found Debbie dead in the closed off carriage. There was a huge amount of blood and she had been stabbed over ten times. The knife slashes were to her face, neck, and abdomen and her hands had clear evidence of defensive wounds. Debbie's throat had been cut and there were multiple stab wounds to her breasts. The fatal blows struck her heart. The poor luggage porter who found Debbie's body must have been terribly shaken and upset by his discovery. In no time at all the police were on the scene and detectives were examining the carriage.

Some of the blood in the carriage was felt to have belonged to the attacker - which suggested that Debbie had put up a brave and almighty struggle before she died. The murder weapon (which the police calculated was probably a high quality kitchen knife) was never found. There was no sign of sexual assault - though it could be that the attacker never got a chance to do anything on this front because of the tremendous struggle which ensued. Rape might well have been the initial motivation in the attack but it was not something that transpired in the end. There was still money in Debbie's purse when she was found and none of her jewellery was taken so robbery definitely didn't appear to be the motive.

There were around seventy people on the train at the time of the murder but the fact that Debbie was on a closed carriage obviously meant they were in no position to help. The weird thing is that hardly anyone seemed to hear any commotion. One person who did was an eighteen year-old French woman named Helene Jousseline who was on the train. Jousseline was in England working as an au pair. The French girl said she heard two minutes of terrifying screams shortly after the train left Brixton station. She said she followed a suspicious man when the train stopped at Victoria but then lost him. This man was never identified. We have no idea if he was Debbie's killer or just some innocent passenger who Jousseline latched onto because she didn't like the look of him.

At the inquest into Debbie's death the French girl was criticised for not pulling the communication cord available to passengers - which was designed to stop the train for an emergency. If she had done that the train would have stopped and it would have been very difficult for the murderer to flee without being seen by witnesses. In this scenario he would surely have been picked up by the police. The killer would surely have had some blood on his clothes so it would have been difficult to hide this if he was relatively isolated. Sadly though the killer was not isolated. He was able to blend into the endless throng of commuters who passed through this old station.

You might think that it would be rather difficult to murder someone on a train in broad daylight and then escape from one of the busiest train stations in the country without detection but - sadly - this is exactly what happened. The person responsible for Debbie's murder was never found. The police suspected that Debbie was murdered between Brixton and Victoria because the eight minutes between these stations was one of the longest on that line without a stop. Eight minutes would have given the killer enough time to kill Debbie and then clean himself up somewhat. He must have then sat in the carriage with the dead body as he nervously waited for the train to arrive at Victoria. One would imagine that the killer would have been off that train like shot once it arrived. We don't know if the killer headed for the underground or simply left the station to escape into the busy streets. The latter probably would have had more logic if one were in that situation.

It could be that Debbie was murdered in a tunnel. If the French girl is correct then the struggle between Debbie and the killer lasted for about two minutes. Today it would be impossible to do something like this because trains do not have closed carriages and they also have extensive CCTV systems. If you murder someone on a train today you WILL be caught on camera and you will not get away with the crime. In 1988 though that sadly wasn't the case. One should note again that the busy nature of Victoria station probably made it easier for the killer to get away. A quarter of a million people passed through the station each day in 1988 so it would have been relatively easy for the murderer to lose themselves in a crowd.

When the body of Debbie Linsey was discovered, the police temporarily ordered all trains on the Victoria line to be cancelled and stopped. They questioned thousands of commuters in a desperate attempt to extract any relevant information that might capture this brutal killer. The police established that Debbie must have been killed about thirty minutes after she first boarded the train. This fact obviously helped them to get a good idea of where the train was when the murder took place. Of the seventy people who had been on the train when Debbie was murdered, the police managed to eliminate around sixty from their enquires. The remaining passengers though remained unaccounted for. They were like missing jigsaw pieces in this case because the killer must have been among them.

Helene Jousseline told the police that she heard a woman scream in the next compartment as the train went past a part of the line where it was in full view of many houses. The police conducted door to door enquires on this stretch of the line in the faint hope that someone in these houses had seen anything but it came to nothing and was always a long shot. If you live in a house near a railway line you tend in the end not to pay much attention to the trains that periodically roll past and - besides - it would be very difficult to actually see what was going on inside the train anyway. It was a bright sunny day when Debbie was murdered and with the sun on the window of the darkly lit train no one could have seen much from afar.

As for suspects in this case there were a number of potential leads but - frustratingly - none of these led to the case being solved. One witness said they remembered seeing a man get off the train at Victoria with blood on his face. The blood samples the police took from the carriage though were never matched though with any criminal on their files. The DNA database in those days was yet to be established properly and forensic police techniques were less advanced than they are today. Another witness later said he saw a bloodied man at Victoria station washing his face in the toilets shortly after the train Debbie was murdered on had pulled in. In hindsight this was obviously deeply suspicious but it didn't necessarily mean the man in question was a killer.

Complicating matters was the fact that there was a big football match that night (England were playing the Netherlands in a friendly at Wembley Stadium) and a number of football supporters had used the train. Given that football supporters (especially in the 1980s) were known to be obstreperous and prone to fights it could be that the man in the toilets had nothing to do with Debbie's death and was simply a football hooligan. Maybe it was just an innocent man who got a nosebleed. The man in the toilets did not match the description of the suspicious man the French girl had tried to follow. This was obviously frustrating to the police because the descriptions of these suspects was conflicting and not consistent. In short it was simply confusing.

Debbie's carriage was near the front of the train. This meant that once the train pulled in at the station the killer would have been fairly distant from most of the other passengers on the train as they all opened the doors and stepped out onto the platform. The location of the closed carriage in relation to the rest of the train was probably appealing to him for this reason. He knew that he could hop off the train and disappear while many of the passengers (and indeed staff) were still some way back at the other end of the platform.

Perhaps the best lead in this case was a man who was seen getting off the train at Penge East station only to then get BACK on the train via a different carriage. It could be that this man got off the train and then got back in Debbie's closed carriage with the express intention of assaulting her. Getting off the train at a station and then getting straight back into Debbie's closed carriage was highly suspicious and there was probably a good likelihood that this man (if the witness was credible) was the killer. Sadly though, he could not be identified. The lack of extensive CCTV in those days was obviously a hindrance to the police working this case in 1988. While we all find the surveillance festooned society we live in today a trifle sinister at times it does at least make life much harder for criminals and killers.

The police believed that the man responsible for the attack on

Debbie Linsley was probably a rapist who had done these types of crimes (rape that is - probably not murder) before and then ended up killing Debbie when she made a lot of noise and put up much more of a fight than he had anticipated. This made it doubly confusing for the police when they failed to connect the blood samples from the carriage to anyone they had encountered before. It seemed strange to them that someone capable of this crime had never been arrested for anything before. Most killers turn out to have previous arrests for things rape and robbery. That patently didn't seem to be the case with this murderer.

The police reconstructed Debbie's last movements before she got on the train in the hope that this might jog the memory of someone but this failed to dredge up any new information. Debbie had a boyfriend up in Scotland and he was investigated too but proved to have nothing to do with the crime. The extensive search for the murder weapon by police and railway workers also proved fruitless. This was very frustrating because the recovery of a knife would have least have given the police something new to go on. They could have checked it for fingerprints or tried to work out where it had been purchased. Over six hundred people were questioned by the police in relation to this case but no one was charged.

There is a theory that attacker might have known Debbie and tracked her movements that day but the police were not persuaded by this theory themselves and believe it was purely a random attack. No one ever reported seeing a man following or watching Debbie that day as she waited to board the train. Though not impossible (who knows what goes on in the mind of a killer?) it would appear to be rather unlikely that someone was stalking Debbie and decided to kill her on a train in broad daylight. Wouldn't this stalker have found a somewhat safer location to kill Debbie? Why strike in broad daylight on a busy train?

Another theory is that because it was established that Debbie smoked two cigarettes during her train journey, her death might have been the result of an argument that got out of hand. This theory proposes that someone on the carriage asked Debbie to stop smoking and she refused - whereupon they argued and she ended up dead. This theory doesn't really make any sense because they were on a designated smoking carriage so why would someone get offended that Debbie was smoking there? Besides, in those days, people were used to having smokers on trains. It made the trains stink but it was just something you had to put up with.

And why would a commuter be carrying a kitchen knife on a train anyway? Ordinary decent people do not carry dangerous knives around with them. And are we really supposed to believe that a train passenger would stab a woman to death in broad daylight merely because of an argument about smoking? That doesn't have an awful lot of credibility as a theory to explain Debbie's horrendous murder. It seems much more likely that the killer was just a straight up maniac who already had dark thoughts even before he boarded the train. You don't get on a train carrying a kitchen knife if you are a normal person.

Debbie was buried at Holy Trinity Church, Bromley. She was buried in the bridesmaid's dress she was due to wear at her brother's wedding. As a consequence of this shocking murder, British Rail instructed their train guards to patrol all moving trains more often and keep an eye on any lone female passengers to make sure they were safe. Closed carriages, of the type that Debbie was murdered on, were reduced and phased out. The police also advised women not to used closed carriages on trains anymore until they were completely phased out and removed from the lines.

The murder of Debbie Linsley was re-opened by the police in 2002 because by this time they had built up a more complete DNA profile of the offender with new techniques. Despite a reward fund and fresh appeals for information though this brutal and puzzling murder has yet to be solved. We can only hope that one day the killer of Debbie Linsley will finally be brought to justice. As for retrospective suspects in the murder of Debbie Linsley, the name of Robert Napper is sometimes suggested by true crime buffs. Robert Napper was born in Erith, London, in 1966. His childhood was pretty awful and he spent some time in care. He also underwent psychiatric treatment. Napper suffered some sexual abuse when he was growing-up and it is said that this changed his personality and made him feel detached from society.

Like a number of serial killers there is evidence that Napper was a Peeping Tom from a young age. In the late 1980s, Napper told his mother that he had raped someone and she reported this to the police. However no action was taken. It is said that Napper's mother broke off communication with him at this point. In July 1992, Napper murdered Rachel Nickell on Wimbledon Common. Rachel was with her two-year old son at the time and stabbed nearly fifty times. Her throat was slit and she was sexually assaulted. It was a horrendous attack. A man named Colin Stagg was later arrested for the murder but he was completely innocent of this crime and received substantial police compensation. Robert Napper was actually a suspect in the murder of Rachel Nickell but the police, in what was a mistake in hindsight, eliminated him from their inquires. Their misguided focus on Colin Stagg was obviously a tragic distraction.

In November 1993, Robert Napper killed 27-year-old Samantha Bisset in Plumstead by stabbing her multiple times. He also killed Bisset's four-year-old daughter Jazmine Jemima Bisset by suffocation. Napper is believed to have sexually assaulted both victims. Napper mutilated the body of Samantha Bisset in grisly fashion, cutting her open and peeling back skin. He stabbed at internal organs and took away some body parts as a trophy. The crime scene was highly disturbing. Napper had even tried tried to cut one of the victim's legs off. Robert Napper was not exactly a genius when it came to covering his tracks and the police found his fingerprints in the flat where the murders had taken place. He was convicted at the Old Bailey in October 1995 of these two murders.

The police also realised that Napper had been a serial rapist. They believe he was in all likelihood the Green Chain Rapist. This was the name given to a rapist who staged seventy sexual assaults on women in south-east London up to 1994. It didn't seem like a coincidence that the activities of the Green Chain rapist seemed to end once Robert Napper was behind bars. In 2004, new forensic techniques connected Robert Napper to the murder of Rachel Nickell. He was convicted on manslaughter for this murder in 2008 because of diminished responsibility.

Robert Napper has spent most of his time in Broadmoor since his arrest. He believes he can communicate through telepathy and claims he once won the Nobel Peace Prize. Suffice to say, Robert Napper is completely insane. The obvious problem with the theory that Napper killed Debbie Linsley is that one would surely presume the police have his DNA on file? He would have been connected to the murder by now if he matched the blood found in the train carriage. The murder of Debbie Linsley had the hallmarks of Napper but it seems doubtful that he was the killer - despite operating in that general area in that general timeframe.

Sadly, the parents of Debbie Linsley were given any closure to this murder case because no one was ever put on trial for her murder. Debbie was desperately unlucky because she had only gone home for three days and in those three days was murdered. The police said this was an exceptionally unusual crime and almost unheard of in their experience. If you board a busy train in broad daylight the last thing you expect is for someone to get on the train and murder you.

Studies have indicated that serial killers do not have natural emotions like fear and anxiety. As a consequence, serial killers need to do something extreme to experience any feelings at all. Between 30% to 40% of serial killers display abnormal brainwave patterns. Serial killers do not have a rational and logical voice in their head telling them that a course of action is wrong. They will ignore and banish any such thoughts. Killing a person on a train in broad daylight made no sense at all (in terms of risk) but the killer in this case was blind to logic. The murderer of Debbie Linsley just seemed determined to attack someone that day and Debbie Linsley was - tragically - the unfortunate person he zeroed in on. It was just a very strange, unusual, and tragic murder.

THE NEWCASTLE HALLOWEEN MURDER

Halloween night in Newcastle was the scene for a perplexing unsolved murder in 1963. The murder took place in Goldspink Lane in the Newcastle Upon Tyne district of Sandyford.

The victim was 70 year-old Katherine Lilian Armstrong. Katherine was a retired headmistress and spinster who lived alone in a large but gloomy residence known as Doncaster House. She was devout Methodist who often only left her home to go to choir practice. Since retiring from her position at Denton Road Junior School in 1957, Katherine Armstrong had lived a quiet life and mostly kept herself to herself. She was literally the last person you'd expect to be the victim of a brutal murder capable of baffling the police.

Katherine was due at choir practice at 7-30pm on Halloween night but failed to show up. This was most unlike her because - as one would expect of a former headmistress - Katherine Armstrong was always punctual, reliable, and never missed appointments. The next morning, Katherine's cousin Ada Ridley arrived at Doncaster House for a visit. Ada had never liked her cousin living in this house all alone and had tried many times to persuade Katherine to move into a flat closer to other family members.

Katherine was proud and independent though and had always

declined to do this. She said she liked living alone and had no intention of moving out of her house. Katherine was simply one of those people happy with their own company. It didn't really bother Katherine if she didn't talk to many people in the course of her day. Besides, she had choir practice on a regular basis so it wasn't as if she was a hermit or anything.

That chilly morning, the day after Halloween, Ada was rather alarmed when she saw that Karherine's curtains were still drawn shut at 10-30 am. This was most unlike Katherine because she was always up at the crack of dawn and if she had gone out then why had she left the curtains shut? No one answered the door when Ada knocked so she called the police and explained her concerns about the situation. Ada was worried that Katherine might have had a fall or perhaps even suffered a stroke.

When they arrived the police decided to force their way into the house and they were met with a grisly and most unexpected sight. Katherine was dead at the bottom of the stairs. She was clothed with her slippers still on and had a nylon stocking tied around her neck. There were nearly thirty stab wounds on her face and neck and she was covered in bruises. Katherine's hands were covered in defensive stab wounds - which obviously suggested she had put up a big struggle. The police had probably expected to find that the old lady had fallen down the stairs or had a heart attack. The last thing they'd expected that morning was to suddenly find themselves plunged into a grisly murder mystery.

The police were (in equal measure) now to be frustrated and puzzled by the circumstances of the murder. There was no sign of any forced entry to the house and no sign of sexual assault. No one had broken in and no one had to tried to rape or sexually assault Katherine Armstrong. There was also no sign of a murder weapon and no sign of any fingerprints or footprints in the house other than those of Katherine. The police, to state the obvious, had very little to go on. In those days forensics were a far cry from the DNA techniques the police have today so the police in 1963 were further hamstrung by their inability to test the blood and deduce if some of it did NOT belong to Katherine Armstrong. The official cause of death was cited as shock and blood loss. There was a LOT of blood at the crime scene. It was a ghastly and shocking sight.

Because there was no sign of forced entry the police had to be open to the possibility that Katherine knew her attacker and had willingly let them in. This didn't though lead to any significant breakthrough in the case. Katherine didn't know that many people and it seemed rather unlikely that someone from the church choir or her family had murdered her. The murder soon became the biggest ever murder investigation on Tyneside. Police officers and detectives had their leave and days off cancelled so that the case could be investigated around the clock. These police officers endlessly searched bins, ditches, gardens, and drains for sign of the murder weapon (the obvious theory was that the killer may have dropped the weapon as he fled) but frustratingly drew a blank.

One potential lead was a man who had been the chief suspect in the murder of another female pensioner in the area some months before. However, upon investigation, the police could find no evidence that this man had anything to do with the death of Katherine Armstrong. They couldn't even establish if he was in the area on Halloween. The police took two hundred statements from the public and handed out numerous questionnaires on their door to door inquires in the early days of the case. Three months after the murder, the police had questioned 16,000 people and still had detectives working night and day on the case. And yet they still couldn't find the killer.

The police could find no plausible suspect who might have reason to attack Katherine. There were no known violent killers or criminals active in the area at the time. One possibility was that Katherine had interrupted a burglar but why would a burglar stab a 70 year-old woman thirty times? Wouldn't that be overkill? A burglar could surely have just

restrained or incapacitated her in a considerably less
bloodthirsty and messy way. Because she was a former
headmistress the police presumably investigated the
possibility of some embittered ex-pupil attacking her but there
was never any mention of this being a possible line of enquiry.
The police clearly must have found this to be another dead
end.

Katherine's cousin Ada Ridley told the local newspaper that in
her opinion Katherine had been killed by some teenagers who
snuck into her house for a Halloween prank. Ada believed that
Katherine had discovered the teenagers in the house and they
had killed her to stop her from reporting them to the police. If
this was indeed the case then the teenagers must have had
enough knowledge of Katherine Armstrong to know that she
lived alone. A troublesome teenager is hardly likely to sneak
into a house full of family members but MIGHT sneak into the
house of a lone vulnerable elderly person. Whoever did this
crime was despicable and cowardly indeed.

Ada's theory that local hooligan teenagers were the culprits
proved impossible to verify. Contemporary accounts of this
case sometimes suggest that trick or treaters might have been
involved in the murder but trick or treating was definitely not
a thing in the England of 1963. Trick or treating has always
been more of an American tradition. The police, to their great
frustration, could find no credible witness statements
concerning any suspicious people fleeing the scene. Despite
their exhaustive efforts they could not solve this case. We
simply don't know who killed Katherine Armstrong on
Halloween night in 1963 and given the passage of time it
seems increasingly doubtful that we ever will. It does seem
plausible that more than one person was involved in the
murder but we simply don't know for sure what really
happened.

As for who might have killed Katherine, it appears that we can
rule out any serial killer of the era. Besides, serial killers tend
to have a sexual motive (even with elderly people - in fact

some serial killers specifically target elderly people) and was no sign that Katherine was sexually assaulted. The most obvious theory in a case like this would usually be that Katherine interrupted a robbery but in this case nothing was stolen. Once Katherine was dead the robber would have have ample time to ransack the house as it was completely empty of people. It's possible that Katherine had nothing worth stealing but you wouldn't expect a hardened violent robber to kill someone and then quickly leave with absolutely nothing.

This leaves us with the theory favoured by Katherine's cousin Ada. Ada believed that cruel and heartless teen tearaways had broken into the house as a prank or maybe to scare or harass Katherine and then ended up killing her when they were discovered or confronted. One can well imagine that Katherine Armstrong, a former headmistress, would potentially have been very stern and brave in confronting these obnoxious kids and told them in no uncertain terms that she was going to get the police involved. Maybe the kids then turned on Katherine and ended up killing her. It sounds slightly fanciful but cities like Newcastle were not exactly short of feral and dangerous kids in the early 1960s and teenage boys of that era would often have carried knives.

I would favour the theory (with a few modifications) put forward by Ada Ridley as the most likely explanation for what happened that night but - alas - we don't know for sure and probably never will. The last sighting of Katherine Armstrong was by some kids at around 6-30 on Halloween night. What happened between then and the police discovering her body the next morning has never been solved. We know she was stabbed to death but why and by whom we simply don't know.

The murder of Katherine Armstrong was disturbingly cruel and almost inexplicable. It just goes to show you that murder victims come in all shapes and sizes and don't always conform to one specific type.

SPRING-HEELED JACK - THE VICTORIAN DEMON OF LONDON

Spring-Heeled Jack is an alleged supernatural criminal first sighted in 1837 in London. In the volume Encounters with Flying Humanoids, Ken Gerhard describes Spring-Heeled Jack in the following way - "So named because of his apparent ability to bound effortlessly through the air, Spring-Heeled Jack was greatly feared by residents of suburban London during the 1830s. A diabolical, super-villain of sorts, he was usually described as being tall, thin, and cloaked in a tight-fitting oilskin suit, as well as a flowing cape. Jack first gained notoriety when he began to accost solitary, young women by ripping at their clothing with steely claws while he breathed noxious, blue flames into their faces. To this day, no one is sure of Jack's true identity, nor from where this notorious scoundrel came.'

The legend of this bizarre menace began in October 1837 when a young woman named Mary Stevens was walking home from Lavender Hill (where she was employed as a servant). The girl said she was assaulted in an alley by a monstrous figure who ripped at her clothes with claw like hands and had the cold clammy fingers of an animated corpse. Mary claimed that words could hardly do justice to the terrifying nature of this flesh crawling assailant. He was like some ghostly monster with the face of a zombie and bright red eyes that seemed to come from the fiery pits of Hell itself. Mary managed to scream for help during the attack and this brought members of the public onto the scene - whereupon the mysterious and alarming fiend fled into the night in impossible fashion. The beast was not only lightning quick but also elusive. One minute he was there and in the next second he was gone in a flash.

Who did Mary encounter that night? She was deemed to be a credible enough witness when she spoke of her spine chilling encounter with god knows what. Mary wasn't a drunk or someone who was prone to making up stories. She really did seem to have had a strange and bewildering encounter with someone very frightening indeed. And so began the mystery and legend of the uncanny rascal destined to be forever known as Spring-Heeled Jack. The alarming encounter with Mary Stevens was merely the tip of the iceberg for this dreaded fiend. Jack was soon creating mass panic in various parts of England. You might say that, for a time, Spring-Heeled Jack became ubiquitous. He was all over the place.

The next day Spring-Heeled Jack was sighted again by a coachman who claimed that Jack leapt in front of his carriage in death-defying fashion and then made his escape over a wall (a wall that no mere mortal would have been able to scale) with a spine-chilling cackle of laughter before vanishing into the night. Jack, as you've probably worked out by now, got his name because of his reputed ability to leap up into the air - almost as if he was flying.

This famous rascal therefore had what what you might describe as supernatural qualities attributed to him. It would obviously be rather difficult to catch a criminal who had the ability to leap over houses so you might say that Jack was rather elusive - to put it mildly! The legend of Spring-Heeled Jack now had firm roots and began to flourish. In the England of the late 1830s, Spring-Heeled Jack was like Blighty's version of Bigfoot. The actual existence of the fiend seemed unlikely but all the same plenty of people claimed to have seen it.

Illustrations of Jack tend to have him as a scrawny and sinister figure with winged arms. He is usually depicted as looking like a cross between the child catcher in Chitty Chitty Bang Bang and the monster in the horror film Jeepers Creepers. He is usually depicted as having an impish Devil like appearance with a pointed Jimmy Hill chin and red eyes. Jack looks rather like Emperor Ming from Flash Gordon (albeit a less suave version of Ming) in some of the illustrations I perused in the writing of this chapter. Sometimes he is depicted with artificial wings like Batman and sometimes the wings appear to be real wings. The one constant in illustrations of Spring-Heeled Jack seems to be an evil smirk. He obviously got a big kick out of frightening the living daylights out of the general public.

Separating fact from fiction in this legend is not easy though. Was there any truth to this legend at all or is Jack is simply an urban myth or piece of entertaining English folklore? We should remember that people at the time were very prone to believing in the supernatural. Many people still believed in witches and even vampires. Tales of a winged monster who could leap over tremendously high walls were obviously taken at face value by more people in 1837 than they would be today. If you described an encounter with Spring Heeled-Jack today you'd probably be asked why you hadn't filmed him on your phone! It was obviously a lot easier in 1837 to come up with a fantastic story without having to provide too much in the way of evidence.

The two most famous accounts of Spring-Heeled Jack are the Jane Alsop and Lucy Scales cases. In the Alsop case, a young woman named Jane Alsop claimed that she answered the door to a police officer (presumably, the police officer wanted some assistance from Jane's father - that seems to be the general perception) who claimed to have captured the fiend. Jane went out to see for herself if the police officer really had captured Jack (you could say that Jane was rather brave in doing this but maybe curiosity just got the better of her - who wouldn't want a look at Spring-Heeled Jack if given the chance?) - whereupon Jack then threw off his cloak and vomited blue flame as his eyes sparkled a hellish red glow. Jack then fled the scene in his usual magical gymnastic fashion - though not before Jane had seen his hideous appearance for herself.

Cases like this, whether true or not, were enough to get Spring-Heeled Jack in the newspapers by now. Very soon servant girls all over London were swapping lurid stories about this alleged fiend who seemed to enjoy scaring people - especially young women. A man named Thomas Millbank was initially arrested for the attack on Alsop but then set free when it was established he was incapable of breathing blue fire! You honestly couldn't have made that up!

Millbank had actually turned himself in to the police claiming to be Spring-Heeled Jack but he was obviously just some crazy person looking for attention. The fact that Millbank looked fairly normal (no red eyes at all and a normal chin) and patently lacked the ability to leap over houses also rather torpedoed his fanciful claims of being the dreaded and notorious Spring-Heeled Jack! Millbank was set free by the police and after this five minutes of fame and notoriety slid back into the obscurity from whence he came.

Several days later, 18-year-old Lucy Scales also reported a sighting of Jack after visiting her brother in Limehouse. Just as with Jane Alsop, she reported that the creature seemed to spew forth blue flames form its mouth like a Demonic fire-eater. Lucy's sister said that the assailant carried a lantern and was disturbingly monstrous and thin. There were other alleged encounters in this vein. People were soon tripping over themselves to report their own brush with the fabled bat-winged red-eyed troublemaker. As you might imagine, Jack was soon creating quite a stir with him being the subject of so many (and most likely tall) tales. Very soon there were few people in England who hadn't heard of Spring-Heeled Jack.

It is said that parents of this era with obstreperous children would warn them that if they didn't behave they might receive a visit from the sinister Spring-Heeled Jack. Eat up your carrots and do your school work or Jack will pay you a visit! Jack was now becoming a mythic bogeyman - even to children. The legend of Spring-Heeled Jack grew and grew. There were sightings in Sussex and Liverpool and even soldiers and army officers reported encountering the creature at their barracks. Young women would continue to tell stories of how Jack had surprised them in unlit streets and then leapt away in a single bound that took him clear over tall gates or walls.

Jack was now a regular in the news headlines and the authorities began to investigate the case. Legend has it that the Duke of Wellington (who was no spring chicken by now but still clearly spry and brave) even set off on horseback to hunt and shoot the creature. Needless to say he was unsuccessful in this task. Jack soon became a very famous figure and began to appear in penny dreadfuls. He was like a cross between a superhero and Jack the Ripper. A weird folk memory casting a dark and sinister shadow over the present.

So who was this figure? Was it mere folklore or something supernatural? Some suspect that Jack was simply mass hysteria based on a few strange crime incidents where a criminal was embellished to be something ghostly or monstrous. It could be that Jack was simply a tall tale that began to spiral into something more mainstream. This sociological explanation would appear to have a lot of credibility.

A fairly plausible (and therefore more prosaic) explanation than the supernatural theory is that the legend of Spring-Heeled Jack was something which spiraled out of a prank. A young group of aristocrats were suspected at the time of creating the character of Jack and staging the pranks as a piece of mischief to amuse themselves. Aristocrats of the era had a lot of free time and were known to be fond of acting stupidly so this explanation seems far from the realm of impossibility.

There was a curious case in the Spring-Heeled Jack era of a man being arrested for dressing up in a bear costume to scare woman. It could be that Spring-Heeled Jack was a similar (if more theatrical and refined) sort of prank. The Lord Mayor apparently received a letter in which it was alleged that pranksters had a wager worth £5,000 in which they had to scare women dressed in various disguises which included the Devil and a bear costume.

Could it be that this was the true source of the mystery? That didn't explain though why the pranksters harassed soldiers in their barracks. Would a prankster really want to run the risk of being shot by a spooked soldier? The soldiers at Aldershot did indeed claim to have shot at Jack but said their bullets had no effect on this supernatural rapscallion. A bullet definitely WOULD have had an effect on a bone idle aristocrat wearing a fancy dress Devil mask though!

An interesting suspect in this mystery was the Marquess of Waterford. The Marquess of Waterford was a nobleman who was considered to be completely crazy and infamous for not treating women terribly well at times. He was in London at the time of the first sightings of Jack so remains a possible suspect in this legend. Most accounts of the Marquess of Waterford suggest he was probably mad enough to have created the Spring-Heeled Jack hysteria purely as a joke. You might say he was sort of like the Jeremy Beadle of his day. This theory doesn't really explain though why people attributed amazing leaping powers to Jack. How did the nutty old Marquess manage to fake that? A trampoline?

One salient factor in the aristocrat theory is that Jack - despite having ample opportunity by all accounts - never robbed any of his victims. Money was not a motive. Jack was only interested in scaring people. There were endless reports of Jack throughout the Victorian era but the mystery was never solved. It has been alleged that Jack was once responsible for murdering a prostitute but this is obviously impossible to verify.

Some have speculated that Jack might even have been a vigilante (rather like Batman!) who went out at night in an elaborate costume to fight crime. This theory though would appear to ave a rather obvious flaw in that it begs the question of why a supposedly moral vigilante would be out scaring women! The sightings of Spring-Heeled Jack eventually petered out and the fiend became part of Victorian folklore.

Maybe the simplest explanation to this mystery is the one proposed by Mike Dash. Dash, who has written books about unexplained mysteries (from very much what you might describe as a dubious debunker sort of perspective), believes that the legend of Spring-Heeled Jack does not come from history but more contemporary books about folklore. That is to say that Jack is a retrospective creation who was essentially made up years later. Who knows what the real truth is. It could have been a prank or it could have been a deranged criminal. Jack could merely have been the figment of someone's imagination. Maybe it was even - as some allege - the Devil himself!

THE MANCHESTER CANAL PUSHER

The Manchester Canal Pusher is an alleged serial killer said to be active modern day Manchester, England. The killer in question, as his name would suggest, is alleged to randomly push people into one of the many canals in the city's waterways. The legend goes that the mysterious canal pusher has pushed dozens of people into Manchester canals and a large number of these people died as a consequence. The canals in Manchester are surprisingly deep, freezing cold at the best times (let alone alone the winter - when they are ABSOLUTELY perishing), and don't always have spots where you can easily pull yourself back up to safety.

To state the obvious, these canals are potentially very dangerous so if someone unexpectedly pushed you into one at night in the freezing cold you could be in a lot of trouble - especially if you can't swim very well. First of all, you would be in shock and probably panic, you'd be frozen, it might be dark too so you wouldn't be able to see very well, and with all this going on you'd have to find sufficient strength and wits to locate a logical place to pull yourself back up to dry land. What if, on top of all of this, you had just painted the town red and were completely sozzled and drunk to boot? You really would be in desperate trouble wouldn't you?

The canal system stretches for about ten miles through the

heart of Manchester. If you spend time in the city centre you are never too far from this water system. Those canals are all over the place. The legend of this alleged killer gained fresh traction in 2015 when The Daily Star (admittedly not the most high-brow or believable of publications) published a two page article about the mysteriously high number of deaths attributed to Manchester's canals. The basic thrust of the article was that 61 people had died in the canals since 2006 and this was highly suspicious because (so went the gist of the article) surely not all of these deaths could have been mere accidents. What if someone was deliberately pushing them in?

Though crime buffs (not to mention the police) tend to take the Manchester Canal Pusher with a quantity of salt considerably larger than a pinch, it is, to take this mystery at face value for a moment, a very alarming thought to think that someone is pushing people into canals at random. That would make this killer (if we pretend for a moment that they actually exist) one of the strangest and most unusual serial murderers in history. Serial killers shoot people, strangle people, stab people, throttle them with rope, kill victims with hammers, axes, and heaven knows what else but it's hard to think of a serial killer with the MO of pushing people into canals! That would make this killer rather unique and original in the ghastly annuals of murder and true crime.

The Canal Pusher is what you might describe as modern present day folklore in Manchester. Devon has big cats on the moors. Scotland has the Loch Ness Monster. Manchester has a maniac canal pusher. But is this merely an urban legend or something that has any credibility or elements of truth? Among the suspicious canal deaths in Manchester in recent years were that of a young teacher named Nathan Tomlinson. Nathan Tomlinson was found dead in the River Irwell around Christmas time after a night out. This incident could not be put down to alcohol because Tomlinson - on the tragic night in question - had been in regular text contact with his mother and was plainly not drunk. Those who were with him say he was drinking shandy and perfectly in control of his faculties.

When his body was found in the canal his wallet and possessions were missing - which obviously suggested robbery could be a motive.

The difficulty in this case is in separating suspicious deaths like this from the Canal Pusher legend. It is obviously the case that ordinary crime, as in all cities, exists in Manchester. People, sadly, sometimes get mugged, robbed, beaten up, and even murdered in cities. And sometimes, especially if that city has an extensive waterway system, they may end up floating in a canal or a river. It could be that the Manchester Canal Pusher is a case where some of the understandably distraught relatives of those who died in the canals are desperate to find some reason for the loss of a loved one that goes beyond a random accident. They can't believe that their lost relative could simply have fallen into a canal and died. They need a more meaningful explanation to get full closure.

In another case, a young student named David Plunkett was found dead in the Manchester canals in 2012 after a night out. Though his death was ruled an accident his family begged to differ and alleged foul play. They claim that in his last phone message he seemed to be in distress and perhaps was even being attacked. It is cases like this in which the legend of the Canal Pusher has taken root (however precarious that root might be) and refused to ever completely go away. As long as people occasionally die in the Manchester canals then the speculation about the dreaded Canal Pusher will also have some fuel to stay lit. And people are always going to die in canals just as they die in rivers or drown at sea. Tragedies and accidents with bodies of water will always occur.

Former Detective Chief Superintendent Tony Blockley, who believes the Canal Pusher legend is pure fiction, argued that it was highly unlikely a serial killer would choose pushing people into canals as a method of murder because they would have no firm guarantee that the victim would actually die - thus leaving them vulnerable to potential witnesses. Serial killers, as a rule, tend to be rather more ruthless and careful when it comes to tidying up loose ends like this. If you are a serial killer the last thing you want to is leave a wake of victim survivors in your trail. You are likely to end up in prison pretty fast if you do this all the time.

Blockley noted that survivors who have come forward to speak of a canal 'push' attack in Manchester are almost (but not quite - as we shall see) non-existent. The lack of witnesses is an obvious weakness in the case for the existence of this alleged killer. If some lunatic were roaming around Manchester pushing people into canals then you'd probably expect more people to have come forward by now to say it had happened to them. As Blockley noted, pushing people into canals as a method of murder would leave a lot of survivors so you'd expect more of these survivors to have piped up by now if the Canal Pusher was real.

The Manchester Canal Pusher was even the subject of a recent Channel 4 documentary and gained some (short-lived credibility) when Professor Craig Jackson, head of psychology at Birmingham City University, appeared to suggest the killer might exist. In academic crime circles this was clearly like declaring a belief in UFOs or reptilian humanoids from the 4th dimension and Jackson soon did an about turn and said he had been misquoted. The local police in Manchester said that Jackson probably got the canal death figures for Manchester muddled up with drownings in the whole of Greater Manchester - thus making the data invalid and misleading.

The police say that all the deaths in the Manchester canals in recent years have been investigated and in the cases were there was foul play people have been arrested. There is, the police insist, no lone crazed serial killer pushing people into canals on a regular basis. The robbery motive is obviously a factor in some of these incidents. Put yourself in the position of a robber. What better way to escape the crime scene than to push the robbery victim into a canal! That method would ensure no one could chase after you or follow you or quickly alert the police or other members of the public to the crime.

You'd have to be pretty nasty and cold-hearted to do this as the victim could potentially perish as a consequence but violent robbers and muggers (especially if they desperately need money for drugs) tend not to be famed for having a very good moral compass.

It has even been alleged that the Canal Pusher is someone who getting revenge on annoying cyclists for hogging the narrow canal footpaths of Manchester. The obvious weakness of this theory is that it doesn't explain the incidents where people without a bike ended up in the canal! And surely, even the most crazed anti-cyclist would draw the line at pushing cyclists into a canal. They'd be well aware that sort of conduct was not only dangerous but liable to land them in a police station.

The interest in the Canal Pusher was reactivated (again) in 2015 when a cyclist (who was only identified as 'Tony') claimed he had had a frightening encounter with this alleged killer. The cyclist said that he was cycling by a stretch of canal in Manchester when he was suddenly pushed into the water (bike and all) by someone. When he tried to pull himself out of the water the Canal Pusher kicked his hand away and tried to stop Tony from reaching dry land. This story got headlines in the media because here at long last was an elusive witness. We finally had an alleged victim of the Canal Pusher willing to speak. Tony was like the Manchester version of someone in California who goes on the news to say they nearly ran over Bigfoot in their car while driving past the woods.

The cyclist claims that he eventually managed to reach a spot where he could climb back up to safety and by this time his assailant had fled. Though he provided a description of the Canal Pusher the assailant was never recognised or captured. The argument for the theory that the Canal Pusher is real comes not just from eyewitness evidence like that provided by the cyclist Tony but also from the fact that a suspiciously large number of people have died in Manchester's canals in recent years. Manchester, in comparison to London, has far fewer people and a smaller waterway system, and yet - in relative terms - has had more people (pound for pound) die in its waters than London. The question is whether or not this is suspicious or can be explained by other means. There are factors which would lean towards explanations that have nothing to do a phantom Canal Pusher.

Many would claim that the large number of deaths in Manchester's canals are explained by their proximity to the city nightlife (it's not difficult to imagine a scenario where a drunken person staggering home past the canals after a heavy night out in the city centre might accidentally fall in after stopping to urinate) and also the lack of protective barriers in many spots. If a drunk person is staggering and tottering past a dimly lit canal with no barriers at some unearthly hour then it probably isn't the greatest surprise in the world if they fall in by accident from time to time. You can add in too the traditional Manchester cobbles - which can be slippy in the rain or winter.

Pete Marsh, a Detective Superintendent of Greater Manchester Police, said that 85 canal deaths were thoroughly investigated by the police and that nearly all of them had definitive and 'natural' explanations. Out of the seventy-seven canal deaths in Manchester since 2007 the authorities consider only twelve of these deaths to be suspicious and difficult to explain. To give an example, people have been fished out of the Manchester canals and found to have died of head injuries or stab wounds. Deaths like these were obviously murders. Most of the people fished out the canals were boys or men. This tends to go against the Canal Pusher theory because boys and men are most likely to fall into a canal (be it through kids playing about or people falling in drunk after a night on the town) than girls or women.

It should be noted again that the local police say The Manchester Canal Pusher is an urban myth and doesn't actually exist. They point out that all cities with waterway systems (like Amsterdam for example) experience tragic deaths in canals. Some conspiracy true crime theorists though have argued that this could be the police suppressing what they actually know in order not to create a panic! It is often said that one thing which makes the existence of the Canal Pusher dubious is the fact that this alleged killer has never shown up on CCTV anywhere. Manchester has an extensive CCTV system (in fact, in terms of cameras per person it is one of the most surveillance heavy cities in the world) and yet the Canal Pusher has remained elusive. It could be that the killer (should he exist) has a lot of knowledge of the local area and always chooses to operate in places where is a blind spot in the camera system.

The real truth of the Canal Pusher is impossible to say for sure. The killer could be a local myth or there REALLY could be some lunatic randomly pushing people into Manchester canals. Given that most of the canal deaths are dismissed as accidents then this killer - should he exist - has got the greatest protection of all in that the police don't believe he exists! The existence of The Manchester Canal Pusher is open to question but, just to be on the safe side, if you ever visit Manchester and stroll past a canal late at night it might be a good idea not to get too close to the water's edge - just in case the Canal Pusher is lurking nearby...

IDENTIFICATION BY SEVERED HEAD - THE TATTINGSTONE SUITCASE MURDER

On the 6th of January 1967, a 17 year-old warehouse worker from Muswell Hill named Bernard Michael Oliver vanished seemingly without trace. He had been out with some friends but when he didn't return his father called the police and reported him missing. Bernard was described as a gentle soul with a low IQ. He was a meek character and had the mental age of a child. This obviously made his disappearance all the more worrying for his relatives. It was completely out of character for Bernard to go away without telling his family.

He had been missing for ten days when this case took a tragic and gruesome twist.

A farm worker named Fred was out in his tractor in a field near the village of Tattingstone in Suffolk when he noticed two suitcases that had been dumped on the ground behind a hedge. Fred decided to stop and get rid of the suitcases (he naturally assumed that some lout had dumped them there to get rid of some rubbish) but curiosity clearly got the better of him because before he did this he opened them up to see what was inside in the cases. What the farm worker found in the two suitcases was beyond horrific. They both contained human body parts.

Bernard Michael Oliver had been expertly chopped up into eight pieces and placed within the suitcases. His severed head was among the body parts. The police deduced that the murder of Bernard had taken place about forty-eight hours before his remains were found. A post-mortem revealed that he had been sexually assaulted before he was murdered. The method of murder was strangulation. One of the two suitcases used to contain the remains had the initials P.V.A. and a laundry mark reading QL 42 was found on one of the hand towels found with the remains. What did these initials and numbers mean and would they be any help in finding the killer? One other detail was that Bernard's jacket pocket was found to contain a brand of matches which were only made in Israel. This suggested he had consorted with some well travelled people.

Bernard had been partially stripped naked before being dismembered and placed in the suitcases. A weird detail was that his nails had been manicured and the post-mortem revealed that he had been well fed right up to the point of his death. He'd even had a recent haircut. Whoever murdered Bernard had been looking after him well - right up to the point of the murder. That was not completely unheard of for a killer (or serial killer - Dennis Nilsen, to give a random example, was kind to his victims before he strangled them) but still slightly strange.

Try as they did, the police could not identify the body so they took the morbid and unusual (but sadly necessary in this case) step of releasing a photograph of the severed head in the hope that anyone might know who the victim was. The head was propped up with open eyes and a scarf was used to hide the bottom of the neck where the severance had taken place. As best they could in these awful circumstances, the police tried to maintain some semblance of dignity for the deceased victim.

When the picture was released the family of Bernard Michael Oliver eventually came forward and confirmed that - sadly - the victim was Bernard. One of Bernard's brothers later said it was a devastating loss that the family never came to terms with or recovered from. The death of a loved relative from natural causes is bad enough but to lose someone in these circumstances was absolutely shattering. It was the sort of thing you never expect to happen. The worst nightmare of any family.

The police were never able to establish where the murder and dismemberment took place but they believe that it probably occurred in Suffolk rather than Muswell Hill (where Bernard was from). The police investigation into Bernard's death was begun by the Suffolk Police before being handed over to the Metropolitan Police. Some 2045 statements were taken in the first four months of the investigation. The police investigated the markings on the suitcases and hand towel but failed to come up with any conclusive leads as a consequence. This was obviously very frustrating because they were desperate to solve this awful murder and bring Bernard's killer to justice.

Because of the skilled and tidy way in which the body had been dissected and packed away the police worked on the presumption that the killer (or indeed killers) might have some medical knowledge or training. In cases like this the police can usually tell if the dismemberment was done by a medical professional or an amateur. Occasionally there must be cases where a killer with medical training makes the dismemberment look more haphazard than he is actually capable of for the purposes of misdirection but - generally - the police tend to know when a killer has had some surgical or medical training. The instinct of the police experts in this case was that the person who cut up Bernard Michael Oliver knew what he was doing. This was no amateur.

There were apparently some alleged sightings of Bernard in Muswell Hill during the time he was missing - which added to the mystery. Was the killer with Bernard in London during the time he was supposed to be missing? Could it be that Bernard (who was not the most streetwise of teenagers) had sensed no danger from the person who killed him - until it was too late that is? A woman in Tattingstone would later tell the police that she saw a man carrying a suitcase in the village on the night that the cases were left in the field. She said the man wore a hat, was middle-aged, and had a trench coat on. He was described as very smart looking and carried himself with what you might describe as an urbane air. The urbane air of a medical professional? It seemed possible.

The police knocked on every door in Tattingstone investigating this case and also conducted inquires in the closest villages. There were a number of suspects in the police investigation into Bernard's murder. One prime suspect was a doctor named Martin Bruce Reddington who once had a practice in Muswell Hill. Reddington was wanted by the police for the indecent sexual assault of young males and had fled to South Africa. It is said though that he returned to England on a regular basis. A private investigator would later claim that the markings on the suitcase in the which the victim was found could be traced to three men in Muswell Hill - and one of these was Reddington. The private investigator was pretty sure that Reddington was involved in this murder and that he probably didn't act alone.

On the face of it, Reddington was a pretty good suspect. He

had connections to Muswell Hill, preyed on young men, and had medical training. However, despite all of these suspicious connections to the case he was apparently never questioned by the police because they could not find sufficient evidence linking him to the crime. The police were not willing to press charges until such time as they had a case that would stand up in court and this situation never arose.

A major stumbling block was the fact that the police couldn't even prove that Reddington was in England at the time of the murder. Reddington was arrested by the police in Australia a decade later for sexually assaulting a young man. He died in 1995. All the evidence suggests that Reddington most likely had a hand in Bernard's murder. There are simply too many coincidences and connections linking him to this case and when stacked as a whole they seem impossible to ignore.

Another intriguing suspect was another doctor - John Roussel Byles. As with Reddington, Byles was known to sexually assault teenagers. He was also a child molester. There seems to be compelling evidence that Byles was the head of a paedophile ring. Byles moved to Australia in the early seventies and was arrested for sexual assault there. After skipping bail he committed suicide in 1975. Here's the thing though - one of his suicide notes was to Reddington and the two men were both police suspects in the 1973 murder of a boy in London. Case closed? We don't know for sure but Reddington and Byles would appear to be excellent suspects in this terrible and wicked murder.

In his suicide note, Byles told the police he regretted what he had done but did not refer specifically to the murder of Bernard Michael Oliver. The date of Byles' suicide was close to the anniversary of the death of Bernard. Coincidence? It appears to be more than plausible that Reddington and Byles were the killers in this case. The frustrating thing though is that there was never a trial. We never got to see these two men placed under scrutiny in a court of law. Would they have cracked in police custody and confessed all? Would they have blamed one another? Would they simply have maintained their innocence and fought a winning case with a shrewd QC? Those questions will sadly never be answered now.

Another person of interest in this case was Joe Meek. Meek was a producer involved in the record industry and lived in Islington. He had a connection to Bernard Michael Oliver because Bernard had apparently once had a job stacking tapes in his studio. Only weeks after Bernard's death, Joe Meek killed himself at the age of 37 after murdering his landlady with a shotgun. Meek was known to be gay and had a conviction for propositioning a man at a public toilet. In those more unenlightened days being gay was virtually a crime. It is alleged that Meek was fearful of the police questioning him over Bernard's death and this anxiety was supposedly a factor in his suicide. It seems doubtful though that it was guilt which prompted Meek's hand. He simply didn't want the hassle of having to go through police interviews. Meek's heavy consumption of amphetamines was said to make him prone to violent and unpredictable mood swings.

The argument against Meek as a suspect is that it seems doubtful that he would have had the ability to cut up the body so expertly. His suicide was generally felt to have been a consequence of financial woes more than anything. Those that knew Meek say he was suffering from poor mental health by the time of his death. Meek is said to have believed that if he died this would be a good thing because the ghost of Buddy Holly would be waiting for him. Meek does, whether unfairly or fairly, remain one of the suspects who seems fated to forever be linked to this case - however vaguely. It is the fact that Meek knew Bernard Michael Oliver which, more than anything, tends to make him an enduring suspect in this strange case.

The most famous suspect in this murder case is none other than Reggie Kray - the notorious London gangster. The Kray brothers knew Suffolk quite well because they were evacuated there during the war. They also purchased a house near

Tattingstone in 1968 and had already purchased a Suffolk home for the parents. The Krays visited this area even before they bought the houses. Reggie Kray, who was gay, confessed to the murder of a young gay boy near the end of his life and the boy in question is sometimes alleged to have been Bernard Michael Oliver. The truth is though that we simply don't know if Kray's link to this case is pure speculation and coincidence or something more concrete. Even if Kray's confession of murdering a young gay boy is the truth (and Reggie kray was obviously more than capable of murder) that doesn't necessarily mean he was talking about Bernard Michael Oliver. The Kray connections to the area where Bernard was found are certainly intriguing though.

One of Bernard's brothers later said that Reggie Kray would hold parties at the cottage in Suffolk and that rent boys would be brought in for the 'clients' Reggie had invited. Bernard's brother seemed to imply that both he and Bernard had been to one of these parties. In fact, some members of Bernard's family were convinced that Reggie had something to do with Bernard's death. A few days after the discovery of Bernard's remains, the police had visited a cottage in Tattonstone that was alleged to hold 'gay parties' involving seaman and sailors. This evidently did not yield any tangible leads though.

Though the case was never solved the police say that the murder of Bernard Michael Oliver will be looked at again whenever any relevant new information comes to light. In 2012 there was a mysterious (if frustratingly inconclusive) new development when a man reported that he had seen a man wearing medical gloves at Ipswich docks a few days before the body parts of Bernard were found. The man seemed to have two suitcases with him. The witness said he had gone to the police about ten years after Bernard was killed but they hadn't been interested in hearing his statement. He had more luck when he went to the police again in 2012.

The witness said of the Ipswich docks incident - "As we came around the corner we heard a bang. We walked round the corner and there were a pair of main gates and a courtyard where RW Paul offices were. We were right outside the gate and looked through the iron railings. We stopped and looked around to see who was there. There were two suitcases which sat to the left-hand side of the archway and we though 'why would there be two suitcases standing there?' A guy walked from the right, his forearms towards his chest with his hands in the air. He had pink gloves on. I recognised the gloves as it wasn't long after my appendix operation. The figure was frightening. He had a really long, drawn face. The guy was well-dressed with a long black mac-type coat, dark trousers and polished shoes. We ran, bump-started the bike and fled. I can still see that drawn face."

As of yet though this decades old mystery has yet to be conclusively solved. Reddington and Byles would still appear to be the most plausible culprits for Bernard's sad murder. The road where Bernard Michael Oliver's remains were found became known as Suitcase Lane in Tattingstone. For a long time after the gruesome discovery there the locals refused to walk down this road anymore. The family of Bernard Michael Oliver believe the murder was carefully planned and premeditated and that more than one person was involved. They were understandably devastated that - despite national headlines and reward funds - the case was never solved and no one was brought to justice.

There was a strange coda to this case that may or may not be related. A couple of weeks after Bernard was killed, the dismembered body of a fourteen year-boy named Michael John Trower was found at at Waterhall on the Sussex Downs, near Brighton. Michael was said to spend a lot of time on the pier and in amusement arcades and it is believed that he was known by various child sex offenders. There is a theory that the murders of Bernard and Michael are connected and were done by the same people but this has proved impossible to verify and remains pure speculation.

THE BAFFLING MURDER OF JILL DANDO

In the 1990s, Jill Dando was one of the most recognisable and famous faces in Britain thanks to her duties as a newsreader for the BBC. Many more people watched 'traditional' television back then than they do today (in our information overload streaming web obsessed age) and so Jill Dando was very famous indeed. Dando also hosted Crimewatch (a show which highlights unsolved crimes and appeals for fresh information to catch criminals) and the travel show Holiday. Dando had been on Masterchef, The Royal Variety Performance, Blankety Blank, Countdown, Antiques Roadshow, children's television, breakfast television, Noel's House Party, and Points of View. She had also been part of the BBC's election night coverage in 1992 and 1997. Jill Dando was literally all over the place. She was one of the most high profile television presenters in the country and everyone knew who she was. Dando was the BBC's Golden Girl.

On the morning of the 26th of April 1999, Jill Dando was shot dead outside her home in Fulham, London. She was 37 years-old. The killer had shot her in the head (as she put the key in her door to go inside) and then quickly fled the scene. It was a shocking and baffling murder. Why on earth would anyone want to kill Jill Dando? That was to prove a question which rather perplexed the police. One slightly puzzling thing right away was that Dando was rarely at this Fulham house and preparing to sell it. How did the murderer know she would be there that specific day? This suggested that the killer had Dando under surveillance and was closely following her movements. Indeed, there were reports of a smartly dressed man with a mobile phone 'stalking' Dando in the half-hour before her death.

Jill Dando had visited a stationers and fishmongers before she made her way home to Fulham in her Range Rover and then had a conversation with a traffic warden because she'd parked in the wrong place. The killer clearly seemed to anticipate that Dando was going to visit her Fulham home and moved in for the kill ruthlessly and efficiently. It was said that the killer even bent Dando's head down as he shot her to ensure that only a single bullet would be needed and that she would fall quickly and out of sight. Though she was found by neighbours and taken to hospital, Dando had no chance of surviving a bullet to the head at such close range and was officially pronounced dead not long after the incident. This was definitely one of the strangest true crime cases in recent years. A famous television presenter had been gunned down on her doorstep in a manner akin to a mob 'hit' on some poor Mafioso. It was all pretty bizarre and unbelievable.

After a huge police investigation (which naturally dominated the news headlines in Britain) the police arrested a local oddball named Barry George on suspicion of Jill Dando's murder. The police obsession with this man was puzzling to say the least - especially in hindsight now that we know what happened in the years to come. The police simply refused to accept that anyone other than Barry George could be responsible for the murder of Jill Dando. The evidence for adopting this stubborn stance though was not exactly conclusive or overwhelming and this made the police fixation on Barry George questionable to say the least.

Barry George lived about a mile away from Jill Dando. Barry George was a loner with learning difficulties. He was certainly an odd character but being eccentric does not automatically make one a criminal or murderer. If we were to allow the police to arrest all eccentric people purely for being eccentric then half the nation's population would end up behind bars. Most of us are eccentric in our own different ways. To put it in crude and politically incorrect terms, critics felt that the police in this investigation simply decided to 'stitch-up the local nutter' rather than fully explore other possibilities. One might argue that the police were too far short-sighted in this case and too obsessed with making Barry George fit the murder - as opposed to making the murder fit Barry George.

The police case against Barry George was dubious at best. They made great play of the fact that firearms residue had been found on his clothing but this was later proven to be so minuscule that it proved nothing at all. Half the population of London, if subjected to forensic scrutiny, might be found to have a miniscule speck of firearms residue on them simply from brushing against someone on public transport. This type of evidence had never been used to convict someone before and it hasn't been used to convict someone since. It was later established that police firearms officers had been with Barry George at one point in this investigation - meaning the firearms residue could actually have come from them. The police seemed to be going out of their way to pin the murder on Barry George - however vague the evidence might be (and the evidence in this case was VERY vague).

The police believed though that George was a perfect match for the offender file they had constructed to paint a picture of who might have done this baffling murder. They were absolutely determined to convict Barry George - to the point where they adopted too narrow a vision of this case and did not fully explore other credible theories and lines of enquiry. Far too much stock was put in the offender file. The police (rather ludicrously) also noted that Barry George was found to have several newspapers containing articles about Jill Dando in his flat. Given that George was a mentally troubled hoarder with about ten million newspapers in his flat it would have been nigh on impossible for none of these newspapers to mention Jill Dando because she was one of the most famous people in the country. Millions of people in 1999 probably had a newspaper containing an article about Jill Dando lying around in their house. Once again the police evidence proved nothing.

The police theory was obviously that George had become obsessed with Jill Dando and begun stalking her. This is sadly something that does happen - especially to female celebrities. Given that Dando was engaged and due to be married you can see how the police probably came up with a scenario where

George had been angered and upset by this engagement and decided that if he couldn't have Jill Dando then no one would. The police said that George was found to have four copies of the BBC in-house magazine Ariel memorial to Jill Dando in his flat but it's hard to see how this evidence could be used against him. Many people kept newspaper memorials after the death of Princess Diana but it doesn't mean they killed her. Besides, Barry George used to work as a runner at the BBC and it was there (years before Dando was famous) that he started collecting Ariel magazine.

The police believed that, at some point or other, Barry George had met Jill Dando (perhaps he had got her autograph in the street or something?) and become infatuated. This was certainly never verified though. The police found a note in George's flat in which he confessed that he had trouble dealing with rejection and that this made him angry. They believed that this 'confession' was applicable to his attitude towards Jill Dando. Once again though it was more of a theory or hunch than something which had been proven. The specific note in question did not make reference to Jill Dando by name. George could have been talking about anyone (he was once involved in a marriage that collapsed) or just his feelings in general.

The biggest problem with the police case against Barry George is that the murder was highly efficient and seemed to be meticulously planned in advance. It was done very quickly (the bullet was shot into Dando's temple) and the killer was very elusive in rapidly escaping from the crime scene without much detection at all. This all suggested that the killer had done this sort of thing before and was of above average intelligence. Barry George, by contrast, was an overweight shambles of a man who could barely tie his own shoelaces. It beggared belief to think that he would have been capable of this stealth Mafia style assassination.

Jill Dando was killed with a 9mm Short calibre semi-automatic pistol. The cartridge was judged to have been

modified in a workshop to make the gun less noisy
(neighbours of Jill Dando heard her scream but they did not
hear a gun being fired). This was an important detail in the
case because the police believe that a professional hitman
would not have used such a crude weapon. This made them
believe an amateur was involved - thus (in the police view)
solidifying their belief that Barry George was the killer.

One problem with this theory though was that it implied that
Barry George (who was no Einstein) was capable of modifying
a firearm in a workshop - or indeed had the connections to
arrange for this to be done. Both of these assumptions seemed
questionable. The police argued though that Barry George's
old school had a small-bore rifle range which he would
probably have become familiar with. They also pointed out
that George had briefly served with the Territorial Army and
attended the Kensington and Chelsea gun club for a few
sessions in the early eighties.

One piece of evidence which seemed to make it unlikely that
Barry George killed Jill Dando was the fact she was killed at
11-30am. Staff at the Hammersmith and Fulham Action on
Disability centre told the police that on this very morning
Barry George visited their offices at 11-50am and seemed
perfectly calm and normal. How could Barry George have
murdered Jill Dando, fled the scene, crept back to his flat, had
a wash, changed his clothes, and then walked to the
Hammersmith and Fulham Action on Disability centre all
inside twenty minutes? That was clearly nigh on impossible.
Some of the neighbours of Jill Dando reported that they saw a
man walking away in the area shortly after the murder but
when these neighbours viewed a police identification line-up
that included Barry George they failed to point him out.

Barry George was no angel. The police found evidence that he
was something of a peeping Tom and sometimes followed
women. He had been arrested for indecent assault in the past
but these cases did not go to court. In 1982 though he served
some time in prison for attempted rape. George had once

changed his name to Steve Majors (this name appeared to be a mash-up of the actor Lee Majors and his 'bionic man' character Steve Austin) and pretended to be a stuntman. George had nearly killed himself once attempting a motorcycle stunt as his Steve Majors alter-ego. George adopted various eccentric and bizarre aliases in his life. He once went by the name of Paul Gadd (the real name of the disgraced pop star Gary Glitter). In 1983, Barry George had been found lurking in the grounds of Kensington Palace where Charles and Diana lived.

Barry George lived in what you might describe as a fantasy world of his own. When he was younger he once got into trouble for pretending to be a police officer. He also falsely claimed to be the British Karate Champion. George was like a low IQ cross between Aldridge Prior (the hopeless liar) from Viz and Walter Mitty. He was judged to have Asperger syndrome and various personality disorders. And yet the police made no accommodation to these issues. They treated him as if he was a normal person. When he was questioned by the police in relation to Dando's murder it is doubtful that George even grasped the gravity of the situation he was in. His evidence was probably all over the place.

Barry George was the sort of person who had balaclavas, gas masks, and fake replica guns in his flat. He would take photographs of himself with these and pretend he was in the SAS. To state the obvious, Barry George was not the full shilling. This is probably not someone that you would want to live next door to. There was no conclusive evidence that he was a murderer though. Barry George was just a strange man with learning difficulties. He patently needed more care and supervision. In 2001, despite the flimsy nature of the case against him, Barry George was sentenced to life in prison for Jill Dando's murder. It was a conviction which troubled many because the evidence seemed far from conclusive. The conviction seemed precarious and unconvincing at best so it was no surprise that it ultimately fell apart under fresh and persistent legal scrutiny from Barry George's lawyers in the years to come.

After three appeals, the conviction of Barry George was quashed in 2008 and he was finally set free. This now begged an obvious question. If Barry George was innocent then who had really killed Jill Dando? There were a number of other theories. Because she had hosted Crimewatch (a show which is obviously all about catching criminals and solving crimes) there was a theory that an embittered criminal might have killed Dando in revenge. Maybe the show had put someone behind bars or mentioned some criminal or other and this criminal or their associates (or indeed even relatives) had taken revenge by shooting Dando?

While this 'embittered criminal' theory was one that seemed reasonable to investigate it did not seem to yield any great leads or lines of inquiry. There are stories that an intelligence report suggested one of London's most notorious crime families might have killed Dando but the Met Police declined to investigate this lead because their blinkers were too firmly fixed on the shambling figure of Barry George. Whether it was through the disinterest of the police or lack of evidence (maybe it was a combination of both?), the end result was that no criminal was ever seriously or credibly connected to Dando's murder through anything that had appeared on Crimewatch.

A former IRA member named Wayne Aird claimed that Dando had been killed by an IRA hit squad. While the IRA would doubtless have been capable of such an act this claim was never verified or proven. Aird said that a four man IRA hit squad killed Dando in revenge for her activities on Crimewatch. He was serving time in Wakefield Prison when he made these claims. According to Aird the IRA men escaped in Range Rovers and then hid in a London safehouse until the coast was clear. The police clearly did not take Aird very seriously because they declined to investigate his claim. One factor against this theory is the Northern Ireland peace process. At this delicate and historic time would the IRA and its political wing really have sanctioned the brazen assassination of a famous BBC presenter? It seems unlikely.

Another theory was that the killer of Jill Dando was a barman named Joe who lived in Spain. Joe was said to owe money to Kenneth Noye - a criminal who was put behind bars thanks partly to Crimewatch. Joe was said to live among gangster and criminal ex-pats in Spain and in order to clear his many debts agreed to go to London and stage a revenge killing on Dando. This theory was apparently floated by the National Criminal Intelligence Service. Whether it has any credibility or not though is open to question. The identity of 'Joe' was never established or verified. No one knows if he even existed in the first place. This theory is clearly not impossible but remains too vague to have ever gained much traction among the many competing theories concerning Jill Dando's murder.

The most outlandish theory in relation to this case is that Jill Dando was killed because she was about to expose a BBC paedophile ring. It seems rather far-fetched though to think that Dando was killed by celebrity sex offenders and, besides, the stories of an elite 'above the law' paedophile ring made up of celebrities and politicians were largely exposed as fiction thanks to the infamous Carl Beech affair. Carl Beech was the man who claimed he and others had been abused by a secret group of army officers, celebrities, and politicians who were perfectly willing to kill to cover up their tracks. Beech turned out to be a fantasist who was making it all up. Not only that but he had indecent images of children on his own computer. No doubt there (sadly) ARE child sex offenders among the elite and famous but not to the organised extent that Beech and his supporters falsely claimed.

The police had obviously scoured through Dando's past and private life to see if a scorned lover might potentially be responsible and have had a grudge against her but this also failed to provide any notable leads or lines of enquiry. There was no one in Dando's past or private life with any reason or motive to kill her. The police said they investigated about 2,000 suspects in this case - which would obviously have been a very laborious and lengthy task. Despite all the theories the police seemed resolute in their belief that this was a 'lone stalker' type of murder. This is the main reason why they became so obsessed with Barry George. The police built up a picture of the type of person who they thought probably killed Jill Dando and Barry George (unfortunately for him) ticked most of the boxes in that profile.

So who did kill Jill Dando? The most plausible theory concerning her murder is that Jill Dando was killed in connection with the situation in the former Yugoslavia. Dando had fronted a television aid appeal for Kosovar Albanian refugees and only days before she was killed NATO had bombed Radio Television of Serbia's (RTS) headquarters - killing numerous journalists. The general theory then is that Dando was killed in retaliation for the bombing of Radio Television of Serbia's (RTS) headquarters. RTS was like Serbia's version of the BBC - for whom Dando worked. It was an eye for an eye revenge killing (according to the theory).

The 'hit' on Dando was what you might describe as professional in that she was killed quickly and efficiently and the perpetrator fled the scene in fairly swift and elusive fashion. This obviously suggested that the killer was a trained hired professional and not some lone nutcase (like Barry George for example). Arkan, the Serbian warlord, is alleged to have been the person who ordered the hit on Jill Dando. He died though so it would impossible to question him about it now.

Despite the apparent Serbian connection, the Met Police, for reasons best known to themselves, never actually sent anyone to Serbia to investigate and still stubbornly refuse to accept this theory might be true. The investigation into the murder of Jill Dando therefore remains open and the actual truth has yet to be proven. Hamish Campbell, the police officer who was in charge of investigating the Jill Dando murder, still stubbornly insists that Barry George was the killer. It is doubtful that many would agree with him on this. As far as celebrity deaths in Britain go, the murder of Jill Dando remains one of the most shocking and strange. All these years later it still retains many unanswered questions.

THE QUEEN OF SLAUGHTERING PLACES

The Queen of Slaughtering Places is a reference to Brighton in relation to what became known as The Brighton trunk murders. These murders took place in 1934 - the first of which occurring on June the 7th. It all began when a man at Brighton train station noticed a trunk lying around that was apparently unclaimed. When staff investigated the trunk they detected a very foul odour coming from the case and (fearing the worst) decided to call the police. When the police opened the trunk they found the torso of a woman inside. The legs and feet of this murdered woman were then found in another suitcase at Charing Cross Station. Neither the head nor the hands were ever found though and so - sadly - the unfortunate woman in question could never be identified.

In the media the victim became known as The Girl with the Pretty Feet because the police noted that she had the feet of a dancer. Who she actually was though was destined to remain an enduring and baffling mystery. The police estimated that the murder had taken place about three weeks before the remains were found (which would explain the stench). There was evidence that the murderer had some butchery skills because the limbs had been hacked away (which would require a degree of strength and knowledge) and the body parts packed neatly with brown paper bags and string. The pathologist did not believe though that the person responsible had any surgical skills. He evidently felt the dissection of the body was rather crude and not done by a trained medical professional.

The victim was judged to be in her twenties. Tragically, the police deduced that she was pregnant at the time of her murder. Chief Inspector Donaldson, who led the investigation, believed that an abortionist named Massiah was the chief suspect. Massiah was a dodgy and dubious character indeed and given that the victim was pregnant this all seemed to indicate he could possibly be involved. Massiah was put under surveillance by the police but he was not charged with anything in the end. He later moved to London where his abortion clinic (if one could call it a clinic) soon claimed the life of a woman. Massiah evaded prosecution for this though (he was only removed from the General Medical Register in 1952 - and that was only because he had failed to resubmit his details) and later moved to the West Indies.

It could be that the lack of any medical knowledge apparent in the dissection of the body made the police reluctant to think that Massiah was involved. A more obvious and salient factor was that there was apparently no clear evidence that the victim had undergone any abortion procedure at all. The initial theory concerning Massiah was that a botched abortion had gone wrong and he had disposed of the woman's remains to cover his tracks and hide her death. There was simply no evidence for this theory though. In fact, the evidence suggested Massiah was innocent.

One curious mystery though in this case was that one of the legs of the victim was found to have some olive oil on it. At the time surgeons used olive oil in hospitals to stop profuse bleeding but olive oil was not really used by the general public at all. It was only decades later that olive oil became a staple item of British kitchen cupboards and supermarkets. The olive oil clue never yielded any great breakthrough though. The presence of olive oil did not necessarily indicate that a doctor was involved in this murder because at the time the public could - if they so wished - obtain olive oil in chemists.

A more retrospective suspect in this case is a man named George Shotton. Shotton was posthumously named as the murderer of his wife Mamie Stuart at the inquest into her

death in 1961. Stuart's disappearance and death became
known as The Chorus Girl Murder. Her body was found
dismembered and dissected - which fitted the MO of the killer
in the Brighton trunk murder. Shotton was a bigamist with a
violent temper. He was not a very nice man at all. Shotton was
released from prison in 1922 - so would have been on the
outside when the Brighton trunk murders took place.

Shotton's movements and places of residence indicate that he
spent most of his time after prison flitting between London
and the south coast around the time the trunk murders took
place. This would (vaguely) put him in the right ballpark area
when it comes to people who might potentially have murdered
the suitcase victim. Given that he dismembered his own wife
too one can see how you might plausibly build a case for
George Shotton being involved in the trunk murder. At the
very least you could say that he was an interesting potential
possible suspect to throw into the hat. It has never been
proven that Shotton was involved in the Brighton murder but
there is plenty of circumstantial evidence to connect him to the
case.

In the course of their investigation into the Brighton trunk
murder the police obviously scanned through the list of
current missing persons (specifically women) to see if this
might shed light on who the mysterious suitcase victim might
be. This would, bizarrely, lead to the discovery of another
(though seemingly unrelated) trunk murder. The victim in this
fresh case was identified as 42 year-old Violette Kaye - who
was a prostitute in London. The police learned that Kaye had
gone missing after an argument with the man she lived with.
This was a 26 year-old nightclub bouncer named Toni
Mancini. Mancini was obviously now a person the police were
very interested in speaking too.

Mancini had told Kaye's relatives she had gone to Paris. They
even received a note from her alleging to be in Paris but it was
established that this letter was actually posted in Brighton.
There was obviously some dodgy charade going on and you

didn't need to be Sherlock Holmes to suspect that Toni Mancini was probably behind it all. Mancini had killed Kaye and put her body in a trunk. He then used this trunk to prop up a coffee table in his lodgings. You can probably imagine how foul the smell must have been in the end. Visitors to Mancini's lodgings soon began to complain that the place stank to high heaven.

Mancini had then tried to fool Kaye's relatives into think she was alive and well and living in Paris by forging letters. Kaye was apparently a prostitute AND a dancer of some sort. Maybe her family never knew she was a prostitute and simply thought she was a dancer. This might be why Mancini had chosen Paris as her fictional location. Paris probably had more dancing jobs than anywhere in the world in the 1930s. Mancini was questioned by the police over Kaye's disappearance and so decided to flee. He was arrested in south London and in the meantime the police searched his lodgings and found the body of Violette Kaye in the trunk. This was the second trunk murder the police had stumbled upon in no time at all.

Kaye was judged to have been killed by a violent blow to the head - most likely from a hammer. The blow was so ferocious it drove a piece of bone into her brain. Mancini told the police that he found Violette dead on her bed and that one of her clients (lest we forget she was a prostitute whom men visited on a daily basis) must have killed her. Mancini said he was worried he might be wrongly suspected of the crime and that was why he had fled. His defence was weak to say the least. You'd have got long odds against him avoiding prison at this stage in the investigation.

Mancini was tried in Lewes Assizes. The case appeared on the surface to be pretty open and shut but the expected formality of this trial didn't go according to plan for the prosecution. This was in no small way thanks to Mancini's shrewd QC Norman Birkett. Birkett cast enough doubt on the case to make a conviction surprisingly difficult. It was an impressive display from a legal point of view because Birkett didn't seem to have that much to work with but still managed to tie the prosecution up in knots.

Birkett pointed out that Kaye had traces of morphine in her system when she was discovered. He suggested that she was a drug addict who, in her addled and confused state, fell down the stairs and banged her head. Birkett proposed that the injured Kaye had then managed to crawl back to her bed - where she finally perished. That theory took a lot of swallowing (especially the second part) but it actually seemed to work. After five days Mancini was found not guilty. It wasn't that the jury felt it was impossible for him to have killed Kaye but merely that they didn't think the prosecution had mounted a convincing enough case to prove that this happened.

In 1976, when he was at death's door, Toni Mancini told the News of the World that he HAD killed Violette Kaye after a violent argument. Mancini said that he had thrown a hammer at her and it hit her in the head. Despite his tabloid confession he was not convicted or retried though. There were stories that he might be prosecuted for perjury (he'd obviously lied through his teeth at the original trial) but nothing came of this in the end. All in all, it was a pretty bizarre coda to what was already a pretty bizarre set of murders. Despite the strange fact that the police had encountered two trunk murders in no time at all, Mancini was felt to have nothing to do with the first murder. It was pure coincidence that through investigating one trunk murder the police had quickly stumbled into another! Truth really can be stranger than fiction sometimes.

Believe it or not, these two cases were not the first trunk murders to be connected to Brighton. On the 13th August 1831, a fisherman had found the limbless and headless body of a young woman on a footpath leading from Preston Manor. The woman and her unborn baby had been stuffed into a trunk. The murderer may have assumed that by removing the head that the victim would not be identified but he was wrong in this assumption. The diminutive nature of the torso allowed the police (with help from the locals) to deduce that this was

Celia Holloway - a local woman who was only 4'3 tall. Celia was married to a man named John Holloway. John Holloway suspiciously fled when Celia's body was found but he was soon picked up the police and quickly confessed to the murder.

John Holloway was a bigamist, thief, scoundrel, and murderer. He'd taken up with a woman named Ann Kennett and left Celia destitute - despite the fact she was pregnant. He'd been in prison before and a previous child with Celia had been stillborn. John Holloway was a drunk who was known to knock Celia around. He'd been ordered to pay Celia two shillings a week by a court so she could look after herself and the baby she was expecting but John Holloway had no intention of doing this. He decided instead to murder her to save himself the money. Under the pretext of a reconciliation, he lured Celia to his lodgings and strangled her with rope. His mistress Ann Kennett almost certainly conspired in the murder. It is said that Holloway had second thoughts about the murder at one point but Kennett made sure he went through with it.

After the murder John Holloway burned Celia's clothes and hung her body up in a cupboard just to make sure she was dead. Then he cut up Celia's body and packed it in a trunk. With the use of a wheelbarrow he then disposed of the body in a place that was called Lover's Lane. In this particular case that name was darkly ironic. Celia's family had never never liked John Holloway and always thought she should have nothing to do with him. It's a great shame she didn't take their advice. Celia is said to have loved John Holloway and was blind to the danger he posed. She is once said to have remarked though that if she was ever murdered it would almost certainly be John Holloway who committed the crime. In this prediction she proved to be tragically accurate.

John Holloway plead not-guilty in court but he didn't have a leg to stand on and his case was pretty hopeless. He was found guilty and hanged at Horsham on December the 21st 1831. His body was put on public display to deter anyone else who might

have any thoughts about murdering their wives and sticking
them in a trunk. As for Ann Kennett, she was acquitted and set
free. Though there seems to be little doubt that she was an
accomplice, John Holloway's evidence concerning her was so
contradictory and inconsistent that it was deemed impossible
to establish what exactly her role in this tragic affair had
actually been. As for Celia, well, at least there was some dignity
to her final resting place. Celia's other body parts were
eventually discovered and she was buried in the churchyard of
St John's at Preston. A plaque in her memory was then placed
on the wall.

THE GHOULISH BODY SNATCHERS

There was once a time in Blighty when digging up fresh
corpses from the graveyard and selling them to hospitals and
universities was a pretty lucrative business. Strange yes and
certainly not legal but also true. The most famous exponents of
this grisly practice were Burke & Hare. William Burke and
William Hare were two men from the north of Ireland who
became infamous for their macabre activities in Edinburgh in
1827 and 1828. These two men became close friends when
they moved to Scotland to work on a canal. Burke abandoned
his family when he left Ireland and went to live in Scotland
with his mistress Helen McDougal. Hare lived very close by
and eventually ran a boarding house with Margaret Laird.
Hare and Laird were not officially married but most people
presumed they were man and wife. As for the boarding house,
well, this is definitely not a place you'd want to end up living.
As we shall see, this was what you might describe as the
boarding house from Hell.

Near the end of 1827, one of the residents of the boarding
house died of old age and Burke and Hare came up with a
ghoulish way to recoup the money the old man owed in rent.
That was rather inconsiderate of him to shuffle off this mortal
coil with rent arrears! Hare in particular was pretty furious
about this. Along with Burke, he came up with what he

believed was an ingenious way to make money. Grisly and ghoulish yes but definitely something that had the potential to make them a nice little earner.

They took the dead and still fresh body of the deceased boarder to Edinburgh University where anatomy lecturer Professor Robert Knox was more than happy to take it off their hands. At the time there were strict laws about using corpses for medical research and training medical students. Medical schools and universities could only use the corpses of prisoners, street orphans, or suicides in such research. As a consequence of this there was a chronic shortage of cadavers for medical students and professionals to train and teach with. Hospitals and universities were desperate for dead bodies and willing to pay decent money to get them. Burke and Hare were more than willing to cater to this demand.

Professor Robert Knox paid Burke and Hare seven pounds for the corpse of the perished boarding resident and the two men quickly deduced they might have stumbled across a lucrative - if grim - new business idea. Early in the new year, another resident of the boarding house began to show signs of illness and Burke and Hare took great interest in his ailing condition because they anticipated having another corpse to sell to Professor Knox. They weren't willing to wait and, after losing patience with the man's obstinate refusal to kick the bucket, decided to hasten the poorly man's departure from this vale of tears by suffocating him. They chose this method of murder because it left the corpse undamaged. A corpse with no injuries was much more highly prized by medical schools and universities. Burke and Hare had now graduated from ghoulish opportunists to full fledged killers. Blinded by greed and money, they were now capable of anything.

After selling the corpse of this second (and this time MURDERED) man to the university, Burke and Hare were rather frustrated and annoyed by the pesky good health of other residents in the boarding house. They decided therefore to take matters into their own hands and began luring people to the boarding house so that they could kill them and then sell the body! The greed and ruthlessness of these men was apparent when they killed an elderly woman and her blind grandson. It is believed that Burke and Hare killed around sixteen people in all although the true figure is felt by most to have probably been higher than this. They received between seven and ten pounds for the corpses they sold to the university. When you tally that all up, Burke and Hare collected a tidy sum indeed for their murderous and unusual business activities.

The two men got so greedy and desperate for corpses in the end they even killed a relative of Burke's mistress Helen McDougal. Street prostitutes were also among their victims because these were easy targets and not always likely to be missed by anyone or even reported as missing. Burke and Hare found that, when it came to dead bodies for universities and hospitals, demand far outstripped supply and this made them increasingly desperate and ruthless in their attempts to plug the shortfall and increase their profits. It was a simple equation. The more dead bodies they could supply the more money they would make.

Problems arose for this wicked duo though when medical students at the university began to recognise some of the corpses they were using in their training and studies! These included a few prostitutes and also a children's entertainer named James Wilson. By this stage there was also friction between Burke and Hare. Burke began to suspect that Hare was not sharing the money fairly and maybe even killing people alone for extra profits. As a consequence of this he started taking in lodgers of his own to kill! They say there is no honour among thieves (in this specific case I suppose you might say there is no honour among graverobbers!) and that was definitely true of Burke and Hare. Frazzled by the macabre and illegal nature of what they were doing their nerves must have been increasingly shot by this stage. Paranoid and fearful, they no longer trusted one another.

The last victim of Burke & Hare was Marjory Campbell Docherty. Her body was stored at Burke's house but it was discovered by other lodgers named James and Ann Gray. Helen McDougal tried to bribe the Grays into keeping silent but they declined this offer and bravely went to the police. Burke and Hare, along with Helen and Margaret Laird, were all arrested. Amazingly, Hare was offered immunity to testify against Burke because the prosecution didn't feel they had a huge amount of evidence with which to build a case. This brought protests from the family of victim James Wilson. At the trial, Hare tried to give the impression that he'd had nothing to do with the murders and that William Burke was the driving force behind them. He would say that wouldn't he?

Helen McDougal was released at the end of the trial while Margaret Laird served a short prison sentence. These two women were despised by the public and had to slip into obscurity for their own safety. William Burke was hanged at Lawnmarket on the 28th of January 1929. The judge ordered that his body should be donated to medical science and publicly dissected. You might say the judge (not unreasonably) considered this punishment to be cosmic karma. Burke's skeleton is now on display at Surgeon's Hall in Edinburgh. William Hare was released in February 1829. He fled to England and essentially vanished. As for Professor Robert Knox, he was rather disgraced by his association with Burke and Hare and was more or less drummed out of the academic and the medical establishment in Scotland. He never spoke about the case and eventually opened a medical practice far away in London.

People who (for better or worse but definitely WORSE in this case) blaze a fresh trail in a specific field tend to attract imitators or copycats and so it was with Burke and Hare. The most famous of these copycats were a group known as The London Burkers. They are believed to have murdered at least five people in the 1820s and 1830s. The London Burkers included four men - John Bishop, Thomas Williams, Michael Shields, and James May. This gang was inspired by Burke &

Hare and hit upon the idea of selling corpses to hospitals and medical schools as a way to make money. They sold the corpses to St Bartholomew's Hospital, St Thomas' Hospital, and King's College School of Anatomy.

Corpses were desperately needed in these institutions in order to teach students about human anatomy and give them something to train with. Cadavers were hard to come by so if you could supply a teaching hospital or place of medical learning with fresh undamaged corpses they were more than happy to pay you good money in return. This led to macabre cases like Burke & Hare and the London Burkers (aka The Bethnal Green Gang). It was the grisly era of the body snatchers. The London Burkers began stealing bodies from graves to sell to hospitals but in the end they found that demand exceeded what they could supply.

One of the problems was that the Burkers couldn't just rob any old grave. Hospitals and universities only wanted fresh bodies that had not been damaged in any way. This meant that fiends like the Burkers had to strike fast after a funeral and hope that the body was intact and fairly pristine. All these factors made it doubly difficult for grave robbers to find enough suitable corpses to make their distasteful business flourish in the fashion that they desired. They say money is the root of all evil and that was certainly the case with these men. Their inability to meet the demand for fresh corpses led them to cut out the middle man (which in this case was the cemetery!) and simply resort to murder.

John Bishop said he might have stolen over 500 corpses from graves during his time in this ghoulish business. The end of the Burkers began in 1831 when Bishop and James May delivered the body of a boy to the King's College School of Anatomy. One of the teachers at the school examined the body and found it suspicious. It was almost too fresh. The teacher deduced that the body hadn't even been buried or treated by a doctor. This raised alarm bells because if it hadn't been buried or attended to by anyone then that suggested the boy had been murdered. The Burkers (as they would later become known) were arrested on suspicion of murder.

The deceased boy was never actually identified. The police thought he was an Italian boy named Carlo Ferrari but the Burkers said he was a Lincolnshire farm boy. They couldn't both be right. When the cottage rented by John Bishop was searched the police found possessions and items which suggested that the Burkers had murdered more than one person. Bishop and Thomas Williams both made a confession to the police. They said they had drugged and drowned the boy whose body they took to King's College School of Anatomy.

The men also confessed to other murders. A victim named Frances Pigburn was apparently someone they found sleeping rough in a ditch. Another boy they murdered was also found sleeping rough. The Burkers would promise these people somewhere to lodge. The victims were sedated with a laudanum laced beverage and then drowned in a well. Bishop and Williams were hanged at Newgate in December 1831. A very large crowd numbering thousands turned up to watch. James May was sent to Australia as a convict for his lesser part in the crimes. The confessions of Bishop and Williams obviously made it easier for the other men to maintain their innocence when it came to the murders although they were still clearly grave robbers.

The Anatomy Act of 1832 came about as a result of this and other similar cases. The Anatomy Act provided for the needs of physicians, surgeons, and students by giving them legal access to corpses that were unclaimed after death – in particular, corpses of those who had died in hospital, prison, or a workhouse. The act also meant that next of kin could donate a deceased relatives to medical research in return for the cost of burial. What this all essentially meant was that it was easier for hospitals and universities to find corpses to do teaching and research with. The age of the ghoulish grave robbers was finally over.

When it comes to grave robbers in general true crime (that is to say cases not confined to Blighty) the most famous of all remains Ed Gein. You can't talk about graverobbing WITHOUT mentioning Gein. It's almost impossible! Ed Gein was born in La Crosse County, Wisconsin, on August 27, 1906. Although he killed more than one person, it was Gein's proclivity for ghoulish grave robbing that made him infamous.

Gein was especially close to his mother Augusta Wilhelmine - a bond that would leave him in a mentally fragile state when she died. The family lived on an isolated 155-acre farm in the town of Plainfield in Waushara County. Ed Gein, and his brother Henry, only left the farm to go to school. Their mother was deeply religious and very strict. The two boys were not encouraged to make friends and had it drummed into them that the world was a wicked place they should avoid as much as possible (lest they be infected by its evil).

George Gein, the father, died in 1940. Ed and Henry had to do more on the farm after his death and Ed also picked up work as a sort of handyman around town. Ed Gein was considered to be rather odd by the locals but seemed essentially harmless. He was even used as a babysitter on occasion. Henry, in contrast to Ed, eventually started to find life on the farm dull and constrictive. He had met a woman and planned on moving out. Henry felt that Ed's relationship with their mother was becoming unhealthy.

In 1944 there was a mysterious tragedy when Ed and Henry were burning vegetation on the farm and Henry was later found dead. However, there were no burns on his body. It was presumed to be heart failure or suffocation from the fumes but - retrospectively - it seems very plausible that Ed might have killed Henry. Henry is said to have angered Ed by comments he made about their mother - a fact which supplies the most likely motive.

Now it was just Ed Gein and his mother left on the farm. Gein was devoted to his mother and waited on her hand and foot.

Her health began to collapse though and she endured a stroke. Augusta Gein died in 1945 and Ed Gein was left alone on the farm. He was absolutely devastated. Gein's already fragile mental state rapidly deteriorated. He boarded up his mother's rooms and the house began to grow increasingly dirty and squalid. Gein found himself becoming fascinated with gruesome pictures and Nazi imagery. He continued to work as a handyman and even sold some land so money wasn't a huge problem.

On the morning of November 16, 1957, Plainfield hardware store owner Bernice Worden vanished. Her son, Deputy Sheriff Frank Worden, entered her closed store and found evidence of a robbery. The register was open and there were signs of blood. Worden knew that one of the last customers had been Ed Gein. He'd come in for some antifreeze the night before and said he would return in the morning to collect it.

The police decided to visit the Gein farm and what they found soon became one of the most macabre legends in the history of crime. Searching the property, they found Bernice Worden's decapitated and mutilated body. The police also found human skulls, bones, chairs made of human skin, female genitalia, facemasks made from real faces, and all manner of gruesome mementos. Gein had been digging up bodies in the local cemetery and mutilating them, using the skin to craft bizarre clothes, masks, and furniture. It was quite literally like something out of The Texas Chainsaw Massacre (which of course the Ed Gein story partly inspired).

Under questioning, Gein confessed to stealing nine bodies from the local graveyards. He had been trying to make a 'skin suit' to wear in a deranged bid to feel close to his late mother. Gein also told the police he had killed Mary Hogan, a woman who had been missing since 1954. The head of this woman was found on Gein's farm. The police who worked this case were deeply shocked and affected by the grisly discoveries. They would never forget the awful sights that greeted them on Gein's farm.

On November the 21st, 1957, Gein was arraigned on one count of first degree murder in Waushara County Court, where he pleaded not guilty by reason of insanity. Gein was diagnosed with schizophrenia and found mentally incompetent, thus unfit for trial. He was sent to the Central State Hospital for the Criminally Insane, a maximum-security facility in Waupun, Wisconsin, and later transferred to the Mendota State Hospital in Madison, Wisconsin.

Gein's farm later burned down in what was believed to be an accident rather than deliberate. It was perhaps for the best. The prospect of the farm becoming some macabre 'sightseeing' tourist attraction was not something that the locals or the police relished. Gein died at the Mendota Mental Health Institute in 1984. He was 77. Ghoulish memento collectors chipped away at his gravestone for keepsakes. Gein's unfathomable crimes have remained darkly fascinating over the decades and spawned a number of films loosely based on his exploits. Not just The Texas Chainsaw Massacre but Psycho, The Silence of the Lambs, Deranged, In the Light of the Moon, and many others.

THE THAMES TORSO MURDERS

The Thames Torso Murders are sometimes called the Thames Mysteries or the Embankment Murders. This was a series of unsolved murders that took place in London between 1884 to 1889. We don't know if one single killer was responsible for all the Torso murders. It seems far from impossible though. The thought that another deranged killer was at large in the Ripper era is unavoidably both chilling and morbidly fascinating. Though this case is fascinatingly bizarre and horrendously gruesome it was rather overshadowed by the Jack the Ripper murders and doesn't seem to be famous as it should be. Where it not for Jack the Ripper one would imagine that the Thames Torso Murders would be considerably more famous today.

Could it be though that the Thames Torso Murderer and Jack

the Ripper were one and the same? That theory has been floated by crime buffs - though they are by no means united on this. The general perception seems to be that the Torso killer and Jack the Ripper were probably not the same person but - as ever with historic true crime - we simply don't know for sure. If the Torso killer was a separate entity from the Ripper then he presided over an even longer reign of terror.

This case consists of an escalating series of gruesome discoveries in London relating to body parts. Only one of the victims was ever identified. Because the remains of the victims were often found in water this made it even more difficult to identify them. The killer in this case is attributed with a rather ghoulish sense of humour in that he seemed to be leaving the police a most grisly and unusual puzzle to solve.

At one point in the investigation the police seriously considered the possibility that the culprit was a gang of medical students doing this as a prank with body parts they'd swiped from their university. In the end though it became apparent that this wasn't a gang of mischievous medical students with a black sense of humour. These were real murders. What ultimately ruled out the student theory was a determination by the police pathologist that these bodies were not hacked up for medical purposes (that is to say they did not come from universities or teaching hospitals). There was evidence though that the right arm of one victim had been tourniqueted. This DID suggest that the killer had some medical knowledge.

In 1884 the skull of a woman was found in Tottenham Court Road. The skull still contained some flesh. In Bedford Square a human arm was found wrapped up like a parcel. Then a human torso was found. Medical examinations suggested these body parts were all of the same person. The next victim was found in Rainham in June 1887. The first inkling of this murder was grisly indeed because workers found a female torso wrapped up in paper. The rest of the body had been cut off and some of these body parts were later found in other places. It was an exceptionally macabre and odd thing for anyone to do - even a serial killer.

The police naturally suspected that whoever did this might possibly have some medical training - though they didn't know for sure. They felt it was more likely to have been done by a butcher. The killer was very macabre. At one point the police found a woman's scalp floating in the river. The killer even threw some body parts over the wall of the estate belonging to Mary Shelley. This is what you might describe as ironic because she was the author of Frankenstein.

Just over a year later there was similar find in what became known as The Whitehall Mystery. The remains of a woman were found in three different places. An arm and shoulder were found near the Thames. Then a human torso was found in a vault. In a grisly and macabre touch, the torso was dressed in a petticoat. There was naturally a lot of speculation about this find in relation to Jack the Ripper but the police did not believe the two cases were connected.

You can definitely see why though that comparisons were drawn and the two cases were alleged to be connected by some observers. It seemed like a big coincidence that two savage and depraved killers of this magnitude could both turn up in London at around the same time. The method of death in the Torso killings was obviously hard to establish given the lack of heads, decomposition, ad water damage etc. The best guess was blunt force trauma (given the lack of stab wounds).

As what happened to the heads in this case, no one knows. There is a theory that the killer might have kept the skulls as a memento of his murders. It could be that he simply destroyed them by way of fire. Less than a year later there was a similar case when various body parts of a woman were found scattered around numerous places in London. The body parts included hands, internal organs, and the abdomen. The police identified the victim as a prostitute named Elizabeth Jackson. This was despite the fact that the head was never found (which would obviously have made identification more easy if it had turned up). It was a childhood scar that led to identification in this specific case.

In September 1889, a police constable found a female torso under a railway arch at Pinchin Street, Whitechapel. As before, various body parts were scattered in different locations. The torso showed signs of mutilation and indicated that the victim had been beaten before death. The identity of this last victim was never established. This murder was especially interesting because it took place in the hunting grounds of Jack the Ripper. Was this a coincidence or did the Torso killer do this deliberately? Were they one and the same person all along? There were some similarities to the MO of the Ripper but the police still remained unconvinced and believed this was a different killer.

It seemed like no coincidence that this gruesome find was near identical to the other 'torso' deaths in London in the previous few years. The perpetrator of these gruesome crimes was now known as The Torso Killer. There were at least two other cases in London around of this time of body parts being discovered - which suggests that the killer (if there was one single Killer) might have killed as many as six people. As this case was never solved and completely overshadowed by Jack the Ripper the true facts are impossible to know for sure. There were doubtless many violent murders in London at this time but the connective tissue (if you'll pardon the expression) in these disturbing cases seem too much of a coincidence to ignore. If there really was a single serial killer responsible for these murders the identity of that killer seems destined to remain a mystery.

Those who believe there is a link between the Thames Torso Murders and Jack the Ripper have noted that there were indeed some interesting similarities. In both cases the killer seemed to have a degree of medical or butchery knowledge. The killer in these two cases also shared an interest in mutilation, removal of organs, and patently had a savage hatred of women. There is a theory that the killer could have been a mad doctor or medical student who escaped from an asylum. While that sounds like the plot of a schlocky Vincent Price film on the surface you never know. Stranger Things have probably happened! The killer in this case was very brazen and bold. At one point he left some remains in the basement of the building that Scotland Yard were constructing as their headquarters. He clearly enjoyed the sense that he was playing a cat and mouse game with the authorities.

One of the problems in this case is that because most of the victims were never identified it was all but impossible to build up a picture of what sort of people this killer typically targeted. Details like this obviously make it easier for the police (and modern day armchair crime buffs) to build a profile of the killer. One of the victims was a street prostitute and another judged to be someone of fairly high standing (in that her clothes were expensive and her belly was full of food) so, even within the very limited and constrictive data the police managed to establish, there was no consistent pattern to the victims. This made the Torso killer enigmatic and hard to understand to say the least. This killer seemed to lack the sadism and attention seeking qualities of Jack the Ripper. What was the motive for these murders? It didn't seem to be sexual or financial.

There was something weirdly clinical and artistic about this killer. His crimes were like a ghoulish piece of performance art designed at amusing himself.

No one ever wrote the police claiming to be the Torso killer. They had no idea who he really was. What complicated this investigation too was the fact that the murders took place in a geographical area of twenty square miles. This was much larger than the constricted killing zone of the Ripper and gave the police even less chance of finding the killer than they did in the Ripper (who they obviously ever found either) case. The police simply didn't have the resources to solve the Torso murders. Trying to capture Jack the Ripper was enough of a strain on manpower and time alone. Believe it or not, there were estimated to be several serial killers operating in London at the time so it isn't as if Jack the Ripper and the Torso killer were unique. It was Jack the Ripper though who hogged the headlines. His fame greatly overshadowed any other killer who may have been merrily slaughtering his way through London at the time.

Documents only released in 1990 suggest that the police were open to the possibility that one of the later Torso killings might have been the work of the Ripper. At the time the police did not report details like this because they didn't want to create a panic. They wanted people to think the Ripper was gone for good. If the police did at least consider the possibility of an overlap in these two cases though it does beg the question of whether that might actually be what did indeed happen. Maybe these two killers really did get their grisly handiwork muddled up by the authorities!

The main difference between the Ripper and the Torso killer is that the Torso killer tended not to leave the bodies where they had been murdered as the Ripper did. The Torso killer seemed more calculating and organised than the Ripper. The Ripper seemed to derive pleasure from the risk of his activities whereas the Torso killer sought to eliminate such risks. Although the fame of the Ripper endured far beyond his active years (Jack the Ripper remains the most famous serial killer in history), the Torso killer seemed to be forgotten surprisingly quickly by the people of London once his own activities began to peter out. Who this killer was (if indeed it was one lone person) remains a mystery.

Apropos of nothing, there was a similar sort of 'torso' case in the American city of Cleveland about forty years later. The Cleveland Torso Murderer is one of the grisliest serial killers never captured. The killer was active from 1935 to 1938 and killed between twelve and twenty victims. This Cleveland killer killed both men and women. The targets were chosen very carefully in that they were drifters or homeless people so wouldn't be missed. The victims were dismembered and beheaded. The male victims were castrated. Some of the victims had a chemical agent applied to them. The Cleveland Torso Murderer is credited with twelve official murders but may have killed twenty people in all. There is a theory that this may have been the work of more than one killer but the truth was never really established. The famous lawman Eliot Ness was in charge of the investigation to catch the killer.

At one point the killer even left the remains of one victim outside of the office building where Ness worked - simply to taunt Ness. Because the bodies were often found some time after death and many of the heads had been removed this made identification of the victims almost impossible at times. In fact, only a couple of victims were ever identified. The main suspect in the case was Dr Francis Sweeney. It is said that Ness thought Sweeney was the killer. Sweeney was a former medic in the army who had performed amputations in combat. Sweeney also failed a lie detector test when he was in police custody. However, Sweeney was never charged or prosecuted for the murders - apparently because Ness thought there was little chance of securing a conviction.

One thing that complicated matters was that Dr Sweeney was a cousin of Congressman Martin L. Sweeney. Congressman Martin L. Sweeney was known for his dislike of Eliot Ness and wouldn't have taken too kindly to these murders being pinned on a relative. Dr Sweeney was therefore not put on trial. He was bitter at his treatment by Ness and sent Ness threatening letters until he died. A man named Frank Dolezal was actually arrested for the murders and had a confession beaten out of him but it transpired that he was innocent. Dolezal is believed to attracted suspicion because he knew one of the victims. The question of who The Cleveland Torso Murderer really was therefore remains a mystery. All we really do know is that this was an especially disturbed and grisly killer who clearly enjoyed the attention his crimes were affording him. He was one of the deadliest serial killers never to be captured.

There was a similarish sort of 'torso' case in in Germany decades later too. The Saw-Killer of Hanover was responsible for four murders in the 1970s. The murders took place from 1975 to 1977. The victims had their bodies sawn in half or their limbs cut off. However, none of the victims could be identified and this made capturing the killer even more difficult. Although similar grisly murders have occasionally happened in Germany in later decades no one has ever been connected to the 1970s killings or convicted for the crimes.

The remains of the victims were dumped in very public places (or at least places where they would be found quite quickly - a victim's leg, for example, was dumped in the rubbish bin at a girl's school) and so this suggested the killer was enjoying the fact that he was shocking the authorities and public with his crimes. In fact, there were even suggestions that the main motive was to create a panic that he could bask in - knowing that he had caused it all. This was definitely a killer who seemed to crave attention.

The dismemberment of the victims was very gruesome and made it impossible to identify the victims and thus - alas- impossible to find the killer. The police did not believe the killer had any medical knowledge because the bodies were cut up in a crude way. It seemed much more likely that the killer might be a butcher. Some fingerprints were found on the remains but these prints could not be matched to any prints already on police files. The police believe that the victims suffered from dreadful violence before they died. The upper body of one victim revealed that strangulation had been the cause of death.

One strange thing about these murders is that there were both male and female victims. This was quite unusual because serial killers tend to target only one sex (the gender which they are sexually attracted to). The victims were always quite fresh. One interesting aspect to this case is that the police investigated the theory that the killer was digging these bodies up from cemeteries. That theory was ruled out in the end though.

In 1990, in the German town of Isenbüttel, a female torso was
found. A butcher named Olaf Weinert confessed to this
murder. There was a lot of speculation that Weinert, given the
similarities in the MO of the killer, might be the infamous
Saw-Killer of Hanover. However, when the police investigated
they simply couldn't link Weinert to the earlier murders and
dismissed any possibility of a connection. The true identity of
The Saw-Killer of Hanover there remained unknown.

KAREN MATTHEWS - THE MOTHER WHO ABDUCTED HER OWN DAUGHTER

The day on the 19th of February, 2008 for nine-year old
Shannon Matthews began much like any other day. She woke
up early, had breakfast, and left for Westmoor Junior School
at around eight. That afternoon her class was scheduled to
have a swimming lesson at the local leisure centre so Shannon
had an exciting day in store. Shannon stood not much more
than four feet tall and had freckles and blue eyes. She was a
popular child with other kids and liked by all the parents in the
area.

Shannon lived on Dewsbury Moor in Dewsbury, West
Yorkshire. The estate where she lived was known as the
Moorside. The family lived in a small red brick council house
with three bedrooms. The Moorside was a strange place in that
it felt tatty and bleak up close but if one craned up even
slightly it was nestled in a beautiful area of wide open spaces
and green. Years ago many people in Dewsbury used to work
in the busy textile mills but the old industries were all but gone
now. Though the estate had a bad reputation most of the
people there were thoroughly decent and a long way from the
working class caricatures the media sometimes portrayed
them as.

Shannon's mother was the grumpy looking red-haired 32 year-old Karen Matthews. Karen was a rather dumpy woman with a fondness for parka jackets. She would later say that the last time she saw Shannon that morning Shannon had shouted 'love you!' as she left through the front door. There were later accounts though that Shannon and Karen argued that morning and Karen angrily told her not to come back. Karen's account of that morning was naturally very rose tinted purely for the benefit of the police.

Karen Matthews left school at sixteen and eventually had seven children with five different fathers. She came from a big family herself and had several siblings. Karen would sometimes get confused about how many children she actually had in the end - much to the exasperation of relatives. Shannon and one of her brothers had the same father and for this reason Karen always called them the 'twins' - even though they weren't twins at all. Karen Matthews was, to put it mildly, a woman who was easily confused by the simplest of things.

Some of Karen's former partners were inevitably tracked down by the media when Karen Matthews became infamous. None of them had anything nice to say about her at all. They all (rather predictably) suggested Karen liked to get pregnant because she saw that as a means to obtain more benefit money from the dole office. A couple who lived door to Karen in the years before she moved to the Moorside said that Karen tended to view her children purely as bargaining chips. While this was not entirely true (even the social services said that Karen, for all her faults, had a bond with her children), Karen was clearly a selfish woman who sometimes put her own needs above those of her children.

Shannon's father was a 29 year-old man named Leon Rose who lived in Huddersfield. Shannon used to go and stay with Mr Rose quite frequently in the past but when relations between Karen and Rose became tense this contact became less common. Given a choice, Shannon would rather have been living with her father and his girlfriend Tracey Goldsmith in Huddersfield than on Moorside Road with her mother. As the police would discover, Shannon had written of this desire in her bedroom. Karen had two children with Leon Rose and the other child (Shannon's older brother) lived with Mr Rose in Huddersfield. It is believed that Karen Matthews and Leon Rose split up before Shannon was born.

Also living at Shannon's house on the Moorside was Karen's boyfriend - a 22 year-man named Craig Meehan. Meehan worked at the local Morrisons supermarket on the fish counter. Craig Meehan had always assumed he was the father of Karen's youngest child but police DNA tests taken during the search for Shannon revealed that he wasn't. Though he didn't know it yet, the unassuming tabula rasa that was Craig Meehan would soon be a magnet for all the tabloid red tops in the land. With Shannon's brothers and sisters in the house (four of Karen's seven children lived with her), space was at a premium and the Matthews family lived in modest circumstances.

Just after three in the afternoon, Shannon Matthews was dropped off back at her school by bus after the swimming trip to the leisure centre. Shannon, as on any other day, now had to walk home to Moorside Road. This was a walk that usually took her about twenty minutes. Shannon's friend Megan Aldridge thought it was strange though that Shannon's brother was not waiting outside of the school gates for her when they got back from swimming. Shannon's mother usually made sure her brother was there to walk home with her but for some reason this hadn't been arranged that day.

While she was walking home alone after the swimming lesson, a silver Peugeot car pulled up alongside Shannon and the man inside told her to get in. The car belonged to a 39 year-old man named Michael Donovan. Michael Donovan must have been the oldest 39 year-old in the world. He had no teeth and could have easily passed for a pensioner. Donovan was the uncle of Craig Meehan and lived a mile away in Batley Carr. The police believe that Donovan might have picked up Shannon by the school although Michael Donovan later claimed he picked her up nearer the Moorside estate. One would have thought that if Donovan had picked up Shannon right by the school then someone would have seen her get into his car.

Shannon - much to the frustration of the police who had to investigate her disappearance - seemed to completely vanish with no verifiable sightings so one would presume that Donovan picked her up in a fairly quiet spot. Shannon was perfectly happy to get in the car that afternoon. She had met Michael Donovan before and got on well with him. Shannon may have presumed that maybe her mother or perhaps even Craig Meehan had asked Donovan to give her a lift. It is possible that Shannon thought that Donovan had been on his way to see relatives on the Moorside and just happened to chance upon her walking home so thought he would take her the rest of the way. Donovan had very different plans to that though. The Moorside was the last place he wanted to go.

Michael Donovan was a seriously strange man. His real name was Paul Drake. He had changed his name to Michael Donovan in tribute to the character played by Marc Singer in the early eighties science fiction television miniseries V. V was about reptilian aliens (though they look like lizards these aliens have craftily disguised themselves as humans) who attempt a covert takeover of Earth. Michael Donovan was one of the main leaders of the human resistance against these pesky lizard invaders. The show obviously left a big impression on the former Paul Drake.

One of Drake's brothers was named Michael and complained when he heard of the planned name change (he felt, not unreasonably, that having two Michaels in the family was needlessly confusing and perhaps even a mild threat to his own sense of identity) but his protests fell on deaf ears and so Paul Drake became Michael Donovan thereafter.

Donovan was one of nine children. He attended a school for those with learning difficulties and left when he was sixteen. As a youth he was involved in incidents of arson and theft. He

had a battery of jobs as an adult, including a spell as a delivery
driver, and then married a woman named Susan Bird.

At the time of his marriage, Donovan was receiving psychiatric
treatment. The marriage produced two daughters but was not
destined to endure for very long. Bird and Donovan quickly
grew to despise one another. She claimed he was addicted to
painkillers and was erratic and violent. Donovan in turn said
his wife was a liar and that SHE was the erratic and violent
one. Michael Donovan somehow ended up with custody of
their children after the marriage dissolved but soon after
suffered a bad car crash which left him with serious head
injuries. Since then he had lived on disability benefits and no
longer worked.

Michael Donovan was not mentally equipped to look after two
small children on his own and the authorities soon began to
express concern at his situation. The children were eventually
taken into care but Donovan then secretly picked up one of his
daughters from school and drove her to Blackpool. Two days
later he was arrested in a Blackpool bed and breakfast where
he'd been trying to hide his daughter. This incident had
occurred fifteen months before that fateful day when he picked
up Shannon Matthews in his car. Donovan was an emaciated
looking man with short brown hair that was combed forward
into a pudding bowl fringe. His most arresting features were
his huge bug eyes - which made him seem to be in a
permanent state of shock and bewilderment.

Michael Donovan was certainly no stranger to Shannon
Matthews. He was almost (but not quite) even a sort of
relative. Though not related by blood, Shannon thought of him
as an uncle. Six weeks previously, after the funeral of Craig
Meehan's father, Shannon had been seen by other relatives
sitting on Michael Donovan's knee at the family gathering.
This fact, when it came to light, would completely torpedo the
claims by Karen Matthews that she didn't know Michael
Donovan from Adam and would never trust him with
Shannon. Michael Donovan was considered to be an odd and

rather introverted man by many (if not quite all) of his
neighbours and his relatives largely shared this view.

Shannon got in the car with Michael Donovan after he
stopped. He told Shannon that she had to stay with him for a
short time and her mother and siblings would join them soon.
Shannon must have been very confused by this but she didn't
really question it. They then made the short drive to the
second floor flat at Lidgate Gardens where Michael Donovan
lived. Lidgate Gardens was formed of three parallel blocks of
maisonettes. This was a threadbare flat but it was no worse
than the spartan council house that Shannon called home. It
later came to light that Karen Matthews had been seen by a
neighbour of Donovan visiting Lidgate Gardens a few weeks
previously. This eyewitness was very damaging to Karen
because she told the police more than once that she had no
idea where Michael Donovan lived.

When she got in the car, Michael Donovan told Shannon they
could go to the local fair later as a treat. This trip did to the fair
did not transpire though. Donovan later told Shannon that the
thick winter fog meant the fair had been cancelled. While
Donovan was lying about any proposed visit the fair (it was
simply a means to relax Shannon) he wasn't lying about the
fog that night. A thick winter mist engulfed Dewsbury and
made it look like a Hammer Horror fog machine had gone
beserk. While the nine year-old Shannon must have been
rather confused by all of this she clearly trusted Michael
Donovan and went along with his instructions.

The origin of this unusual state of affairs was an agreement
between Karen Matthews and Donovan some weeks before.
Karen had told Michael Donovan to look after Shannon for a
while but keep it a secret and not let anyone know she was
with him. Michael Donovan hadn't just driven to Dewsbury
Moor out of the blue and then randomly noticed Shannon
walking home. He was following instructions given to him by
Karen Matthews. Donovan later claimed he was a very
reluctant participant in all of this but was bullied into it.

The motivation of Karen Matthews was not as clear as it is sometimes portrayed in the media and retrospectives of this peculiar case. She seemed to begin with a vague idea of getting away from her boyfriend Craig Meehan. Donovan offered a way to do that because he said to Karen she could stay at his flat temporarily if she needed somewhere to live. Karen would actually cite this as what happened more than once to the police and even friends but then change her story several more times - much to the dismay of the baffled detectives who had to question her.

In one of her versions of events, Karen said she planned to leave Craig Meehan but then Meehan got suspicious and Shannon somehow ended up trapped at Donovan's house before Karen had a chance to get herself or the other kids there. Karen then embellished this by saying she didn't know where Donovan lived. She would then embellish it further by saying she didn't even know Shannon was with Michael Donovan. Karen Matthews did this a lot when she was in police custody. Karen would tell lie after lie until her stories all contradicted one another and she had no idea what she was even saying anymore.

There was plenty evidence though to suggest that money was the main motivation of Karen Matthews in this curious case. Karen believed that if Shannon went missing then a reward fund would be activated by tabloids and donations - maybe even celebrities. The grand plan of Karen Matthew was that Shannon would safely live with Michael Donovan in complete secrecy until such time as the reward fund for this missing child was established and reached a sufficiently lucrative value. When this happened, Michael Donovan was then supposed to take Shannon to the police station and claim that he had found her in Dewsbury Market. The reward money would then be handed over to Donovan and he would split the windfall with Karen Matthews.

You didn't need to be Lieutenant Columbo to spot some obvious problems with this plan. What was Shannon going to say when she was inevitably asked by the police where she'd been living and who had been feeding her? Shannon would surely just say that she'd been with 'Uncle Mick' and the entire plan would be blown out of the water in an instant. That was far from the only problem with the hoax. Wouldn't the connection between Michael Donovan and Karen Matthews be discovered by the police in the end and make them both highly suspicious? And was any reward money really going to be handed over to someone who was more or less a relative of Shannon?

Michael Donovan would later claim that Karen Matthews told him if he didn't go along with this plan she would destroy his beloved car (neighbours said that Donovan's car was his pride and joy) and get some men she knew with criminal connections to give him a good hiding. Karen's own explanation for what had actually happened, as we will see, changed about half a dozen times - maybe more. Karen Matthews told several versions of what had happened - none of them having much in the way of plausibility. The most ridiculous claim by Karen Matthews - the apex of her mendacity you might say - was that she had no idea who Michael Donovan was and didn't know where he lived. That claim didn't fly very far at all once it was put under police scrutiny.

The inspiration for this missing child hoax involving Shannon is generally believed to have been the Madeleine McCann case. Shannon went missing only nine months after Madeleine McCann went missing. Karen Matthews had noted there was a sizeable reward fund for information leading to the discovery of Madeleine McCann. She had also noted that the McCann family received many financial donations to fund their search for Madeleine. Karen processed all of this information and a plan so stupid it defied belief began to form in her mind. It was poor Shannon who became the unwitting pawn in this idiotic plan.

At about four in the afternoon, Karen Matthews went around

to the house of her neighbour and relative Victoria Saunders and said she was concerned because Shannon hadn't come home from school yet. Karen, so she claimed, wanted to know if Shannon had come round to play with her cousins but Shannon (obviously) wasn't there. Saunders suggested that Karen should give the school a ring and see if Shannon was still there. Karen did this but (again obviously) drew a blank. Karen was following the protocol of a situation like this. She was pointedly letting neighbours and Shannon's school know that she was worried about Shannon. In the circumstances it would be seen as natural behaviour for someone wondering why their child was late coming home. This was, in hindsight, actually all quite shrewd for a woman you wouldn't readily associate with shrewdness of any kind.

The hoax was obviously only going to work if it was officially activated and the police and media got involved. So, at 6.48pm, Karen Matthews telephoned the police and spoke to Detective Constable Christine Freeman. The conversation lasted about a minute and a half. Karen explained that her daughter had not come home from school and that she had checked with relatives and Shannon's friends but they hadn't seen her either. Detective Constable Freeman asked if there was any reason why Shannon would have run away and Karen said there wasn't. There had, according to Karen, been no arguments or anything like that. Karen said that Shannon had a mobile phone but she'd left it at home so there was no way to contact her. Detective Constable Freeman asked if Karen had telephoned the school yet but Karen was one step ahead on this and confirmed that she'd already done this.

It only took a matter of minutes after the telephone call for police officers to arrive on the Moorside and knock on the door at number 24 Moorside Road where Karen lived. The small house of Karen Matthews was searched by police officers - as were some of the houses of neighbours. Karen's boyfriend Craig Meehan and some of the neighbours were very irritated by this because it made them feel as if they were under suspicion. As far as the police are concerned in cases like this though EVERYONE is under suspicion at first. Family and relatives are the first people that have to be checked out and investigated.

In these sorts of cases the first duty of police officers is to thoroughly search the house where the missing child lives and then examine neighbours and close relatives. Detectives call this 'clearing' the ground from under their feet. The immediate family must be ruled out of the equation before the broader investigation is launched. Look at the completely bungled Tia Sharp case of four years later to see why this is so important. West Yorkshire Police could not be faulted that night for the speed and thoroughness of their response to this worrying case of a missing child.

That night in Dewsbury was the coldest of the year so far. It was absolutely freezing as two hundred police officers began a late night search of the surrounding area for any sign of Shannon. "It was thick fog, the temperature was minus four and if this little girl had got lost and spent the night outside she couldn't have survived," said Christine Freeman. "So my first thought was that we were looking for a child who was probably dead." That first night, Karen Matthews soon had friends, family, volunteers, and an escalating number of police officers embroiled on the first of what would be many sub-zero rain lashed wild goose chases.

Karen Matthews did not participate in the search herself on that first night. She went to the supermarket to buy a sat nav system for her neighbour Neil Hyett. Hyett was Shannon's uncle. Here was clue number one that there was something dubious about Karen Matthews. If your child is missing and you are sick with worry do you really go to the supermarket to do some shopping? Karen was behaving in a normal fashion in a situation where one would be anything but normal. Karen - rather improbably - explained her shopping trip by saying that she wanted to rule out the possibility that Shannon had gone to the supermarket but why on earth would Shannon be hanging around a supermarket for hours on end on the coldest night of the year?

Media vans with satellite dishes soon began to dominate the parking spaces on the Moorside. The press corps quickly got wind of this developing story and wasted no time in rushing to the scene to begin reporting. The local press was also naturally giving this breaking story considerable coverage. Karen Matthews was told by the police that she should not make a public statement at this time because she might say something that would put Shannon in danger if any abductor was listening. Karen was told that she should only make a public statement if it was done in accordance with the police. Natalie Murray, Karen's friend and neighbour, was there when Karen Matthews received these strict instructions. She told Karen to listen to the police and let them handle the investigation.

At 7.30pm though, the day after Shannon was reported as missing, Karen completely ignored the police instructions and came out of her house to speak to the camera crews and reporters who had already gathered outside. "Shannon if you're out there please come home we love you to bits we miss you so much," pleaded Karen. "We love you so much. Please come home Shannon." Karen Matthews looked tired and upset. It was probably her greatest performance and one she would never match. Never again would she be quite so convincing in her fictional role as an anguished mother desperate for news of her missing child. Karen had huge red bags under her eyes when she made this first media appeal. She did genuinely seem like a distraught anxiety ridden mother. Karen looked like someone who hadn't slept for weeks as the flashbulbs went off and camera lights probed her tear streaked face. The police were absolutely amazed when they saw Karen Matthews on national television. She hadn't taken any notice of their instructions at all.

Meanwhile, at Lidgate Gardens, a bizarre situation unfolded where Michael Donovan found himself a benign kidnapper (if such a term isn't an ungainly contradiction) with a confused nine year-old hostage. Donovan was at pains to make sure that

Shannon Matthews didn't watch the television news and see herself plastered all over the headlines. This didn't prove to be the most complex task because nine year-olds tend not to be news junkies. Shannon was more interested in watching cartoons and playing computer games. Donovan told Shannon to stay away from the windows and not make too much noise. It wasn't too difficult for Shannon not to make much noise because aside from Donovan she had no one to play with or talk to. She was though allowed to listen to music as long as she kept the volume low or used headphones.

The police had thousands of places to search in the Shannon Matthews investigation. Garages, sheds, abandoned buildings, factories, gardens, construction sites, fields, woodland. Police divers even had to break through thick ice to search the rivers, ponds, and lakes in the area. The police stopped hundreds of cars to speak to drivers and deployed specialist victim recovery dogs. The search for Shannon was the biggest police operation in the county since the hunt for The Yorkshire Ripper. The police got a set of Shannon's fingerprints from school books in her bedroom. This meant that when they searched a place of interest they could do a fingerprint search to see if there was a match. Houses searched by the police were visited by forensic scientists to search for any trace - however tiny - of blood or DNA. The police even put sniffer dogs in the loft when they searched houses. The police also naturally had to investigate hundreds of registered sex offenders in the area - which proved a mammoth task. Those involved in the volunteer effort were rather alarmed to see that a lot of sex offenders seemed to live near the local schools.

When the police found the scrawled message by Shannon on her bedroom wall saying she wanted to live her dad this was something of a red flag because Karen Matthews had painted a very happy picture of Shannon's life at home and said there were no problems at all. Karen said that Shannon was very happy and loved life on the Moorside. Shannon's message suggested otherwise. This obviously meant that Karen had not been entirely truthful in her police interviews. So if she was lying about this what else could she be lying about?

The police had to gauge if Karen Matthews was simply putting a positive spin on her family life (in the way that most people would be tempted to do in that situation) or if her deception was more meaningful. At this stage the police didn't really know what to think. They continued to find Karen Matthews a strange character to deal with but assumed she just had a very low IQ.

A number of perpetrators in true crime cases are good actors. They tend to get found out in the end under prolonged scrutiny but they can fake it surprisingly well at first. Ian Huntley was a pretty good actor. If you saw Ian Huntley on the television news early on in the Soham case you would probably think he was just a normal young man who was concerned about those missing girls. Karen Matthews was not a good actor. Karen's ability to fake her predicament was simply not consistent enough to be plausible. It was naturally her friends, who had the most access to Karen, who first began to experience doubts.

While Karen could make a decent fist of appearing convincing before the cameras for a brief time she simply didn't have the focus and concentration necessary to keep the charade going 24 hours a day. There was something too normal about Karen Matthews. Her daughter was missing and yet she had beer delivered, cracked jokes, played computer games, went to the chip shop, ate crisps, and did most of the things she would have done when her daughter was not missing. There is no uniform reaction to the anguish and anxiety of having a missing child but if there was a uniform reaction it wouldn't be to stuff your face with Monster Munch and dispense comic banter in the chip shop.

It was inevitable that Karen's close friends and the police family liaison officers would begin to pick up on this. The police, to put it in less than tactful terms, did not think that Karen Matthews was playing with a full deck. In their eyes this

mitigated the fact that Karen's behaviour was - given the
circumstances - rather odd at times. This was only a temporary
respite for Karen. Her incongruous attitude was only odd for a
limited window. Karen's oddness eventually stopped being
odd and received a promotion. In the end Karen was no longer
merely odd. She was eventually deemed to be suspicious.

Karen Matthews moved in with Natalie Murray for a time and
so Natalie was able to study the behaviour of Karen more than
anyone (save for Craig Meehan obviously). Natalie was
increasingly troubled by what she saw. She noted in particular
how Karen would do a teary glum faced appeal or interview
but then when the cameras were off suddenly start smiling or
joking. Natalie thought it was weird that Karen almost seemed
to enjoying this unexpected moment in the public spotlight. It
was also deeply weird the way Karen would almost beam with
pride when she saw a news report about the case and declare
to anyone in earshot that her daughter was now famous.

Tracey Goldsmith, the partner of Leon Rose, joined the
steadily growing list of people who were becoming suspicious
about karen Matthews. "Things didn't add up. Karen was
doing TV appearances, doing appeals and smirking. She was
eating in front of the cameras. We couldn't eat because we
were sick to the stomach. We felt we were in a horrible
dream." During the search for Shannon, Karen even had the
family liaison officers run errands to buy computer games for
her and Craig Meehan. She would comment on how 'fit' some
of the police officers were and joke about how losing one of
your kids wasn't so bad because people gave you free stuff out
of sympathy.

West Yorkshire's police training school had been closed so that
the cadets could join the search for Shannon. Around 10% of
the total manpower of West Yorkshire Police was now involved
in the search to find Shannon. The police were making good
progress when it came to their searches. By the end of the case
they had searched 3,000 homes in addition to questioning
1,500 motorists. 800 CCTV tapes and computer hard drives

were examined by the police and 75% of Britain's victim recovery 'body' dogs were deployed. A police helicopter was a constant presence in the sky as it combed the area searching for visual clues. The Joint Air Reconnaissance Intelligence Centre (JARIC) flew over the area to search for any sign of disturbance in the soil. Though they could not say this to the media or volunteers, the police thought that by now they were probably searching for a body rather than a missing live person.

Given that she knew Shannon was at Lidgate Gardens with Michael Donovan, it was a remarkable display of chutzpah by Karen Matthews to front press conferences and radio interviews. The fact that Karen was rather monosyllabic sort of worked in her favour. Her short brief answers to everything gave everyone less to digest or place under scrutiny. It was only really in private that Karen started to raise a few alarms. It was not just her friends but also the police who began to have doubts. Both the police and Karen's friends found it increasingly odd that Karen seemed to display no anxiety at the thought that something bad might have happened to Shannon.

When they tried - as sensitively as they could - to explain to Karen that she should prepare herself for the worst she shrugged off their pleas and insisted that Shannon would be fine. Karen said she was convinced that nothing had happened to Shannon and she would be found safe and sound. Karen's friends presumed this must be some sort of emotional defence mechanism and that Karen couldn't face up to the actual reality of her situation. The only other alternative was that Karen knew something they didn't. "Straight away my gut was telling me something wasn't right," said Natalie Murray. "Karen was carrying on with normal stuff, tidying up the house. It was as if Shannon had just gone to her friend's."

Back at Lidgate Gardens, Shannon was now hopelessly confused. She had a vague idea that her mother and Michael Donovan were now a couple and that he was essentially her new father. Shannon still didn't understand why her mother hadn't arrived yet. What Shannon didn't know was that her mother and Michael Donovan were not planning a future together. They were simply the world's stupidest hoaxers and exploiting her for the purposes of a get rich quick scheme that had zero chance of success. There is some evidence that by the end of her time at Lidgate Gardens, Shannon was so confused she had started to get Michael Donovan and her father Leon Rose mixed up. She kept thinking that she'd been living with Leon Rose rather than Donovan. The police suspected that Shannon was starting to suffer from hallucinations by the time she was rescued.

Michael Donovan's rented flat was quite dingy and not a nice place to be cooped up for days on end. The living room had threadbare brown carpets while the room Shannon slept in was cramped and scruffy with garish pink and light blue walls. Shannon listened to Busted (a boy band) CDs to pass the time and played computer games. Michael Donovan, bizarrely, seemed to have also given Shannon a child's picture book on how to travel safely. This was an ironic choice of reading material to say the least given the circumstances! Life must have been pretty tedious for Shannon at Lidgate Gardens. She missed her friends and going out to play. Shannon was soon desperate to get back to a normal life and go to school again.

Michael Donovan later claimed that Karen had told him he would only have to look after Shannon for a week at most. That period had already elapsed though and this strange saga would drag on for some days yet. It spoke volumes that Karen Matthews seemed to believe that several days was all it would take to establish a lavish Madeleine McCann style reward fund for Shannon and that all it would take to pocket the money would be for Michael Donovan to walk into a police station with Shannon. Did she really think Donovan would then simply be allowed to go home and make arrangements to claim the reward money? Didn't she realise that the police were likely to take him custody and subject him to lengthy interviews?

Shannon was found to have traces of Traveleeze in her system as a result of her stay at Lidgate Gardens. This is a travel sickness medication. Donovan claimed he gave Shannon these pills because she got car sick when they went out but it is alleged that he used these pills to sedate Shannon and make her less likely to escape. The police officers who rescued Shannon said that she definitely seemed drowsy and confused when they found her. Shannon later told the police that Donovan gave her some white pills to take.

Even more concerning was that Shannon was found to have temazepam in her system. Temazepam is a benzodiazepine and works by slowing down the central nervous system (brain), causing drowsiness which helps one fall asleep. Donovan used this medication himself so may well have given it to Shannon. However, tests indicated that Shannon had been ingesting temazepam for nearly two years. This obviously meant that Karen Matthews must have been sedating her own daughter long before she ended up at Lidgate Gardens. Shannon also had traces of the antidepressant Amitriptyline and the painkillers Tramadol and Dihydrocodeine in her system. Whether it was Michael Donovan or Karen Matthews - or a combination of the two - who was to blame, Shannon was slowly being sedated up to her eyeballs.

Donovan's flat was found to have contained an elasticated strap which was fixed to a roof beam through the hatch loft. The end of the strap had a loop on it which could be tied around Shannon to restrict her movements. The purpose of this was to stop Shannon reaching the front door or windows when Donovan was out. The strap allowed Shannon to move around but not sufficiently to actually leave the flat. While the media exaggerated the nature of this (they sometimes gave the impression that Donovan had Shannon constantly tied up as if she was in a medieval dungeon) there is no disputing that it was sinister and weird. There is no doubt that Shannon was essentially a hostage.

Donovan had given Shannon some writing paper and pens so

that she could write to her siblings. None of these letters were
ever posted. It was just a ruse to keep Shannon occupied and
placated. In a letter to her brother, Shannon wrote - 'I am
missing you so much. I will ask Mike to take me to see you.
Ok? I love you so much.' At some point, confused by the potent
combination of her isolation and the drugs she was taking,
Shannon seemed to believe that Donovan was now her father.
'When me and my dad go to Blackpool,' she wrote, 'we are
going to take some pictures of Blackpool seaside and of us.
Love Shannon and dad.'

Blackpool was where Donovan had taken his daughter before
he was arrested for breaching a court order not to contact his
children. He had obviously told Shannon that this was where
they might have to go in the end. Donovan, lost in his own
delusions, seemed to using Shannon as a surrogate for the
daughters he had lost. He was also clearly starting to get edgy
and making vague plans to depart from Lidgate Gardens
should the need arise. Donovan seemed to sense that this
couldn't go on for much longer. He must have been expecting a
knock on his door at any moment.

The fact that Karen Matthews and Michael Donovan were
turning the life of a nine year-old child upside down and
causing her great stress and confusion was not something that
either of them seemed to be very aware of. Karen Matthews
didn't really seem to care if Shannon had to spend months at
Donovan's flat. Her focus was on the reward money rather
than the welfare of her child. Michael Donovan wasn't much
better. While he was doing his best to look after Shannon and
did not harm her, no normal person would have put
themselves in that situation in the first place. And no one with
a heart would have sedated a child or tethered them to an
elastic leash while they went out shopping.

While the police and Karen's friends eventually came to foster
private but indecipherable doubts about this case on the basis
of Karen's strange behaviour, the same could not be said of the
media. They found Karen to be convincing and took her at face

value. No one in the media cast any doubt on Karen Matthews during the search for Shannon. They cast plenty of doubt on Craig Meehan but this proved to be a blind alley. The media were at a disadvantage because they had far less access to Karen Mathews than family liaison officers and her friends. They conducted Karen's mumbling monosyllabic interviews and took this for shock and grief. What they didn't tend to see was Karen laughing and joking away from the camera once the interview was over.

Casting directors say that child actors are difficult to cast because they are fine when they are talking and the focus is on them but tend to drift out of character when they don't have any dialogue and have to stand in the background. Child actors often tend to lose concentration in this scenario. So it was with Karen Matthews. Karen was essentially a child actor constantly drifting in and out of character. When you watch all the footage of Karen Matthews now during the search for Shannon you can even detect a few moments where she is trying not to laugh. Perhaps it is only with the knowledge of what really happened in this case that this becomes more noticeable now.

Detective Inspector Chris Walker, of West Yorkshire Homicide and Major Enquiry team, was another person who became suspicious of Karen Matthews during the search for Shannon. During an interview with him, Walker was surprised when Karen said that Shannon was in a 'nice warm' environment. This was a strange thing to say. How would she know? "It did raise suspicions in my mind," said Walker, "that she had some idea of what had happened to Shannon and at that time there was absolutely nothing to link her to Shannon's disappearance." It was really the fact that Karen seemed to be so relaxed about her situation that baffled the police and her friends. The media got a fairly decent facsimile of a distraught mother but those with more access to Karen Matthews got something very different in private.

The precise day to day details of Michael Donovan's time with

Shannon at Lidgate Gardens have never really come to light. The police, to protect Shannon's privacy, never really said much about that time and Shannon has never spoken to the media (and probably never will). Michael Donovan was grilled about the time they spent together in court and offered what you might describe as a rather idealised and wistful perspective on these strange weeks. Donovan seemed to suggest that Shannon loved it at Lidgate Gardens and never wanted to go home. Donovan was unlikely to say anything else. To do so would have been to shoot himself in the foot. Michael Donovan never harmed Shannon and looked after her as best he could but he was still essentially functioning as a kidnapper in those weeks. Shannon was a hostage who had no real freedom.

One of the reasons why Michael Donovan had not leaped out at the police as someone to investigate as a matter of urgency is that Karen Matthews did not include him in the list of friends and relatives she assisted the police in drafting so that they could assess all the connections to Karen and Shannon. The fact that Karen had left Donovan off the list was obvious misdirection on her part. When the police became aware of Michael Donovan it's hard to say if they then retrospectively considered his absence from Karen's list of connections to be suspicious or not.

It is possible the police assumed that Karen genuinely didn't consider Donovan to be a relative or a friend and so hadn't bothered to include him. It's not as if he was a regular visitor to Karen's house on Moorside Road. It was a combination of both Donovan's neighbours and the T.I.E list that led the police to Lidgate Gardens in the end. The neighbours were the more dominant factor in this breakthrough with Donovan's presence on the T.I.E list merely confirming to the police that they should speak to this man. All these factors played a part but the police would have spoken to Donovan in the end even without any prompting from his neighbours.

The general facts as far as we can establish them in the hoax are that Karen Matthews and Michael Donovan became friendly at the funeral of Craig Meehan's father. Karen claimed (in one version of her story at least - there were several other versions with different details) she had an argument with Craig Meehan at this funeral and ended up in the company of Donovan. Karen arranged to meet Donovan in a cafe later and asked him if he could look after Shannon because she planned to leave Craig Meehan. It was here then that the abduction plan was hatched. Michael Donovan claimed he'd wanted no part of this plan but Karen threatened to set some very violent men on him if he declined to take part.

Karen's own version of these events changed so often in the end though it was hard to keep track. At one point she would use this broad scenario as her explanation. That is to say she wanted to leave Craig Meehan and planned to get the children to Donovan's flat as a temporary escape. Karen said things just got out of hand after that and she ended up in this muddle of people thinking Shannon was missing and didn't know how to tell anyone the real truth because she thought they'd have a go at her. Karen would then do an about turn on this explanation and ridiculously claim that she had no idea where Michael Donovan lived and would never have left Shannon alone in his company. This was an absolutely laughable claim in light of a witness statement which placed her at Lidgate Gardens before the whole abduction farce.

Some of the relatives of Karen Matthews think she was having an affair with Michael Donovan but then got cold feet and turned against him - though obviously not before poor Shannon had become embroiled in the childlike world and baffling schemes of these two idiots. Given the intense mutual loathing that Karen Matthews and Michael Donovan displayed towards one another in police custody and court it was very hard indeed to believe that much in the way of romance could have ever existed between them.

Another theory is that Karen latched onto Michael Donovan because she heard he got some compensation or insurance for his car crash (when they first got to know each other, Karen had asked Donovan if he could loan her £20,000 but Donovan said he didn't have that kind of money). According to this theory, when she realised that Michael Donovan was nearly as poor as she was Karen lost interest in him. Michael Donovan was at least consistent when he told his side of the story. Though, like Karen Matthews, he was not exactly a reliable narrator the basic theme of Donovan's evidence - that Karen had come up with the hoax and dragooned him into it - was one that made more sense than the mishmash of conspiracy theories and wildly conflicting statements offered by Karen Matthews.

Karen Matthews watched a lot of the live rolling news coverage of the search for Shannon. It was a slightly surreal situation because the search was literally taking place outside of her window but she was largely following it second hand through television. Karen got a kick out of seeing herself on television. She got a kick out of seeing Shannon mentioned on television too. We can only imagine what surreal and delusional daydreams Karen Matthews had during this time. Maybe she pictured herself and Shannon on the This Morning sofa when this all blew over. A celebrity mother and daughter.

Body language experts later had a field day with Karen Matthews on those 'faking it' type television shows where experts show you why criminals were lying all along. However, it is very easy to be wise after the event years later. None of these experts were on the phone to West Yorkshire Police in 2008 to suggest that Karen's shoulder twitches, blinks, shakes of the head, and whatever else it is that body language experts look for, were a gigantic red flag. At the time Karen Matthews seemed convincing enough. No one watching her sombre television interviews detected anything dubious or fake about her grief.

On the morning of the 14th of March, 2008, Shannon had been missing for almost 24 days. This day though the police had finally got around to visiting Lidgate Gardens to speak to

Michael Donovan. Although more than one person had contacted the police helpline in the early days of the Shannon case to suggest they investigate Donovan, it is believed that this visit to Batley Carr was only prompted by yet another confidential tip from a neighbour that the police should check him out. When the police looked into Donovan following this latest tip they found that Michael Donovan's relatives had noted he had become very elusive and reclusive in recent weeks. That did not necessarily prove anything but it was potentially meaningful. It was certainly enough to make the police decide to go and talk to him.

Detective Constables Nick Townsend and Paul Kettlewell were the officers who went to Lidgate Gardens that day. They hadn't really expected to find anything. They just wanted to talk to Michael Donovan, cross him off the list, and see if had any information that might be pertinent to the case. Donovan was something of an outsider in the family and connections of Karen Matthews and Craig Meehan but it was possible he might have heard something. But then something unexpected happened. Donovan's neighbour June Batley came out and spoke to Townsend and Kettlewell. She told them she had sometimes heard what sounded like a toddler running around in Donovan's flat above. "That's when my spidey senses really started tingling," said Townsend. "I couldn't believe what I had heard."

The two detectives knocked on Donovan's door at number 26 but got no answer. They heard from the neighbour though that he never answered his door even if he was in. June Batley also pointed out his car parked nearby and said Donovan never went anywhere without his car. This all obviously meant that Donovan was in the flat but simply not answering the door so the two detectives went back. They then heard what sounded like a child's voice say "Stop it! You're frightening me!" By now, Pc Ian Mosley and Pc Matthew Troake from the operation support unit had arrived to provide back-up. A police dog was also there. Neighbours of Donovan said that in time at all there were four police vans on the scene.

The police forced their way into the flat and saw the head of a little girl appear from a bed base in one of the bedrooms. Shannon had been hidden in a drawer under the bed. "I was elated," said Kettlewell. "I couldn't believe we'd found her and she was alive. As we went down the stairs it was like carrying my own child. She was compliant but bewildered. I passed Nick on the stairs and said, 'I've got her!' I still get emotional about that moment now." Donovan was also hiding under the bed. It was Shannon who told the police where he was. Donovan had pushed two beds together so there was room for both of them to hide.

The police constables pulled Michael Donovan out and restrained him. He was jabbering away like a madman and resisting arrest. Donovan complained loudly when he banged his head as they took him away. Neighbours said that as he was taken away he kept shouting that he was ill and should be in a hospital. A few locals shouted some abuse at Donovan because they presumed that he had abducted Shannon on his own and done God knows what to her in that flat. As the police would soon realise though, this case was a whole lot more complicated than that. Christopher Heaps, a neighbour of Donovan, witnessed the drama that day. "I started hurling abuse at him then, cos of all this time we've been waiting for Shannon. The man was whingeing and complaining and telling police 'You're hurting me, you're hurting me'. After that little Shannon came walking out behind him. She wasn't crying or anything."

Kettlewell took Shannon out to the police car where she ended up sitting on a pile of evidence bags. He said he fought back tears as he spoke to Shannon because all the detectives presumed she was dead. To sit here talking to her felt like a miracle. Kettlewell asked Shannon if her mother knew she was here and Shannon nodded. Shannon said her mother had telephoned only two days ago but Donovan hadn't let her speak to her mum. This was potentially killer evidence but it wasn't actually used in the trial. The police soon had plenty of other evidence on this front from Michael Donovan.

Michael Donovan was taken to Halifax police station and was later treated and assessed at Calderdale Royal Hospital. When he was asked if he wanted to say anything, Michael Donovan told the police to go and talk to Karen. That's all he would say. Go and talk to Karen. Donovan had already told PC Matthew Troake "Get Karen down here, we've got a plan" in the police van after his arrest. Karen Matthews now had an awful lot of explaining to do. She didn't know it yet but she was in a considerable amount of hot water. The abduction hoax had fallen apart (as it was surely always destined to do) and now the police had to somehow make sense of this almighty mess. Michael Donovan had wasted no time at all in implicating Karen Matthews in Shannon's disappearance. He had no intention whatsoever of carrying the can for this alone.

It was unavoidably speculated that Donovan saw Shannon as a sort of substitute daughter and this is why he went along with the hoax. During his trial, Donovan put an amazing gloss on Shannon's time at his flat. He'd made it sound like she was on holiday. Donovan seemed to portraying himself as a great parent/guardian. He seemed pained about his failings in these roles in the past. Michael Donovan's computer hard drive was taken away by the police and thoroughly examined after Shannon was found at Lidgate Gardens. Nothing was found on the hard drive to indicate that Donovan had any sexual interest in children. It was completely clean of any illegal or dodgy material.

The camera crews and photographers who had been sent away to other stories now rushed back to Dewsbury to report on the dramatic new developments. It was very rare in cases like this to actually have a happy ending. The photographers and television camera operators expectantly aimed their devices at number 24 Moorside Road and waited for Karen Matthews to emerge and pose for pictures. They wanted to capture this wonderful moment where a mother's joy and relief warmed the nation's heart. That was the expectation anyway.

What the media got was something different. Karen Matthews

eventually emerged from the house with Craig Meehan and posed for pictures but she did not look like a woman full of joy and relief that her daughter had been found. She looked confused and morose. Karen's friends leaned out the window and told her to smile. The smile was awkward and unconvincing when it arrived.

As Karen stood in her front garden under the light bulb glare of the media you could almost hear her brain whirring away. Her thoughts were firmly on Michael Donovan and what he would tell the police. Even the ever deluded Karen Matthews must have known the situation was now looking very bleak for her. At this stage, from what little they could gather, everyone on the Moorside assumed that Donovan was some local oddball who had abducted Shannon and forced her to live with him. The real facts of this case would come as a great shock and cause much anger and confusion. This was especially the case for Karen's friends and neighbours.

Karen's friends and neighbours had just spent a month walking around Yorkshire in freezing winter weather searching for Shannon. They had given up their precious time and made great sacrifices (which included spending less time with their own children). They had all been conned by Karen Matthews. The police and taxpayers had also been taken for a ride. The investigation into Shannon's disappearance had cost millions of pounds and diverted hundreds of police officers and dozens of detectives from attending to other serious crimes. Karen Matthews must have felt the world beginning to close in around her. By now even she must have realised that her abduction ruse probably hadn't been the greatest idea in the world. How on earth was this now going to resolve itself in a way that even remotely resembled the delusional daydreams of Karen Matthews?

Karen Matthews and Craig Meehan had a house party to celebrate Shannon's safe discovery. The little red brick house was soon full of people and alcohol. There was a strange atmosphere at the party though because friends, neighbours, and relatives were confused as to why Shannon had not come home yet. Not only that but there was no news or any updates about when Shannon might even be expected to come home. Karen had certainly made no real preparations for such an event. Karen told them it was no big deal and the police just needed to ask Shannon some questions. Julie Bushby thought it was odd though that the people on the Moorside seemed to be more excited about Shannon coming home than Karen Matthews did. Karen honestly didn't seem that bothered by the delay.

Any hopes people on the Moorside had about seeing Shannon again though were soon to be dashed by a surprising announcement. The police now made Shannon the subject of an Emergency Protection Order. Under section 46 of the Children Act 1989, if the police have reasonable cause to believe that a child would otherwise be likely to suffer Significant Harm, the child may be kept in or removed to suitable accommodation where they may be protected, e.g. a relative's home, a hospital, a police station, a foster home, children's home or other suitable place. Under section 46, Shannon was placed in the care of social services.

With Michael Donovan in police custody, Karen Matthews must have felt like a big net was slowly but surely beginning to close in around her. Despite the unverified rumours of an affair and the fact that they had worked together on this brainless and cruel hoax it would soon became apparent to the police that Karen Matthews and Michael Donovan didn't like each other very much at all. It would be no overstatement to say that Karen Matthews and Michael Donovan absolutely despised one other. Karen Matthews must have realised there was zero chance of Donovan not implicating her in the hoax. Donovan had nothing to lose now.

Michael Donovan's only slim chance of evading a severe sentence was to say to the police that it was all Karen's idea. The police found Michael Donovan's claim that Karen Matthews had been the main instigator of the plan to be credible and believed Donovan was largely telling the truth about this. This evidence aside, detectives found Michael Donovan to be unreliable. They didn't believe much of his other evidence - especially when he tried to pretend that Shannon had loved her time at Lidgate Gardens and didn't want to leave. That was obviously a bit of a stretch on Donovan's part. It's hard to imagine any nine year-old would want to spend their life locked up in a small flat with Michael Donovan away from their friends and siblings.

Donovan, through his lawyer, prepared a statement for the police in which he set out his side of the story. He said it was all Karen's idea and that he was supposed to take Shannon to the police station when the reward money hit £50,000. Obviously though, he had been arrested before the final part of the plan could be carried out. Donovan said in his statement that he'd wanted no part of this plan but Karen Matthews had threatened him with violence if he didn't go ahead with it. Donovan was at pains in his statement to say that he hadn't harmed Shannon and bought clothes, toys, and games for her.

The police had found Karen Matthews to be exceptionally odd at times when Shannon was missing. Now that Shannon was no longer missing they still found Karen to be odd. The police found it strange that when they told Karen that Shannon had been found she displayed all the emotion of someone who had been informed of the whereabouts of a missing sock. Karen did not ask where Shannon had been found (she already knew this of course - unknown to the police) and she did not ask how Shannon was. In contrast to Karen, Craig Meehan did display emotion and cried when he heard that Shannon was alive. When Shannon was found, Karen and Craig Meehan were taken to the police station but not allowed to interact with or touch Shannon. Karen seemed oddly distant and unemotional to the police officers that day.

Karen was required to formally identify Shannon. The police didn't want Shannon to be contaminated by DNA (Shannon was now essentially a human crime scene for the time being) so Karen had to view Shannon behind a one way mirror. Shannon was with a female police officer playing with sme toys. Karen was asked if the girl was Shannon Matthews - her daughter. "Yes," replied Karen. The police had expected Karen to cry but she did not. They had expected her to ask if she could go and hug Shannon but she didn't do this either. Karen didn't question any of the conditions stipulated by the police. She didn't even ask how Shannon was.

The police were equally bewildered by the attitude of Karen Matthews when she was allowed to properly visit Shannon. The police even had to prompt Karen into buying Shannon a gift to take to the police station. Karen showed Shannon little affection when they were reunited. When the next visit was arranged, Karen was nearly late because she insisted on stopping off to buy herself a sandwich. Lunch seemed to be more important to Karen Matthews than her daughter. The police said that Karen Matthews did a lot of clock watching when she visited Shannon. She couldn't wait to get out of there. Karen clearly felt uncomfortable being around police officers. It is no great mystery why this was the case. Karen Matthews would soon have her fill of police officers in the weeks and months to come.

Karen Matthews had to issue a media statement on why her daughter had not come home yet. Her words (whoever crafted them) were well chosen and designed to dampen any speculation about why Shannon had not returned home. Local reporters later said it was amazing how quickly news on this case spread around the area. Dewsbury was now full of rumours that there was something weird about Shannon's abduction and that the family might have been involved. These rumours were astonishingly accurate. The media were obviously giving this case more coverage than ever now because they also sensed that an unexpected plot twist was on the cards.

Karen Matthews tried to blame everyone but herself when the abduction hoax finally came to an end and the police began to ask questions. There was literally no one that Karen wasn't willing to blame in a desperate attempt to evade responsibility and the punishment that was sure to follow. Among those she blamed was naturally Craig Meehan. During the trial Karen even claimed that Craig Meehan had raped her. Various times during her constantly shifting explanations, Karen said that Craig Meehan had come up with the whole scheme himself and made them go along with it. The police never found any evidence though that Craig Meehan knew anything about the abduction hoax. When the Shannon case went to trial, Craig Meehan wasn't even called as a witness let alone a defendant.

Four days after Shannon was found, Karen was interviewed by the police under caution and told that Donovan had implicated her in the abduction. When she was first questioned by the police about these claims Karen said that she didn't know Shannon had been with Michael Donovan. Karen said she had no idea where Shannon was during the search and had never been to Lidgate Gardens. Michael Donovan, insisted Karen Matthews, was a virtual stranger to her. She'd never let any of her kids be alone with such a strange man.

On April the 2nd there was a very grim subplot when Craig Meehan was arrested by the police. As part of the investigation to find Shannon the police had taken away the computers from the house at number 24 in order to see if Shannon had been in contact with anyone online before she vanished. The computer belonging to Craig Meehan was discovered to have evidence of child pornography. Meehan's computer was found to have history of over six hundred child porn searches and the youngest image he looked at featured a four year-old child. Craig Meehan was filmed by camera crews and snapped by press photographers as he left the house with police officers. At first it was assumed that Meehan had been arrested in connection with Shannon's abduction but it was purely the indecent images of children on his computer that prompted his arrest.

Karen's performances in police interviews and the trial were childlike and all over the place. She would simply deny everything and unfurl lie after lie until she could no longer remember the last lie she had told and began contradicting herself with fresh lies. The fresh lies clashed horribly with the previous lies and made a complete nonsense of anything Karen had said in past interviews. The hole she dug for herself got deeper and deeper. Karen's detachment from reality made her ill equipped for all of this scrutiny. It didn't help that her case was impossible. Even if Karen had stuck to one story and been better prepared it wouldn't have made much difference to the eventual outcome.

When the police realised (with the help of Michael Donovan and to a lesser extent Shannon) this case was a strange sort of hoax that Karen Matthews was well aware of it actually made a lot of sense to them because they now had an explanation for why Karen had seemed so odd at times during the four week search for Shannon. Michael Donovan's claim that Karen had come up with the plan as a means to make money explained why Karen had often seemed so relaxed when Shannon was missing. It also explained why Karen had told the police that Shannon was in a nice 'warm' environment. Karen's claim that she had no idea Michael Donovan had Shannon was quickly dismissed by the police once they examined the facts. She had been seen by relatives talking to Donovan at the funeral of Craig Meehan's father and seen at Lidgate Gardens before the hoax by a neighbour.

On April the 4th, Amanda Hyett, 25, and 49-year-old Alice Meehan were both arrested on suspicion of attempting to pervert the course of justice. Hyett and Meehan were Craig Meehan's sister and mother and the police suspected them of some involvement in the abduction hoax. They were released on bail and although never actually charged but rumours still persist that others were involved in this bewildering affair. Hyett and Alice Meehan's proximity to Karen Matthews clearly made them suspicious to the police. In her evidence (or at least one version of it), Karen claimed that Craig Meehan, Amanda Hyett and Michael Donovan had hatched the abduction plot together and forced her to take the blame.

Karen had never displayed any genuine desire to get Shannon home and seemed disinterested in Michael Donovan. It seemed odd to them that Karen wasn't kicking up more of a fuss about her daughter being taken in care. It was also odd that Karen seemed to never talk about the man who had apparently abducted her daughter for a month. Karen never seemed to mention Michael Donovan at all. It was a subject she avoided. Karen's friends Julie Bushby and Natalie Murray decided to contact the police family liaison officer Christine Freeman. Their plan was that the three of them would get together with Karen Matthews and see if they could get her to talk and finally reveal the truth about this increasingly knotty case.

The meeting with Karen, Christine, Julie, and Natalie took place in Batley town centre in a layby. Christine drove Karen down while Natalie and Julie were driven by another police officer. They then all got into Christine's car. They were rather surprised that Karen readily agreed to this summit. This was encouraging though because it suggested that she wanted to get something off her chest. The four women sat in Freeman's car and Natalie Murray got straight to the point.

"Look Karen, I'm not going to beat about the bush," said Natalie. "There's a lot of stuff I've seen you do and say, none of it adds up to me. You know I know there's something going on." Natalie suggested to Karen that she had wanted to leave Craig Meehan and arranged for both her and kids to stay with Michael Donovan. However, she had then gone cold on the idea - but only after Shannon was already there. Natalie pointed out that she'd noticed Karen had sometimes had a packed bag in her hall as if she was ready to leave at any time. Karen confessed to the three women that this was all true. Karen claimed she ended up in this complete mess because she was scared of Craig Meehan.

"I couldn't believe it," said Christine Freeman. "As she

confessed I started making notes." Natalie and Julie had not expected Karen to confess but they were relieved that she had. "I think in the beginning it (the abduction) was about the money," said Natalie. "It was this big plot to get as much money out of the press or whoever as they could. Then when they realised that wasn't going to happen, it became this big spindle of lies upon lies upon lies upon lies upon lies that she just could not get herself out of." Christine then phoned the police station to report on what Karen had said. She was instructed to arrest Karen Matthews and so did this.

Karen Matthews was sent to New Hall Prison near Wakefield. It seemed to come as a great shock to Karen Matthews when she was sent to prison. She had childishly assumed that after her police interviews were over she would be allowed to go home until the trial. Karen's inability to grasp reality was as strong as ever. Michael Donovan was sent to HM Prison Leeds - a castle style institution that Peter Sutcliffe once called home. Karen Matthews and Donovan were still sticking to their stories when it came to the abduction although it was admittedly harder to keep track of which story Karen Matthews was actually telling.

Donovan had at least stuck to his statement but Karen had told half a dozen different versions of what happened ever since she was first interviewed by the police. Karen's story now seemed to be that it was all Michael Donovan's idea. She claimed she didn't care about any reward money and that she didn't even like Donovan or know him very well and would certainly never have left her beloved daughter with him. Karen had gone full circle with her defence by now. She was now almost back to her original line where she claimed she didn't really know who Michael Donovan was and had no idea where he even lived. None of Karen's many and varied explanations felt like they would withstand too much scrutiny in court at all.

The trial of Karen Matthews was set for the 11th of November at Leeds Crown Court. Karen was to be jointly charged with Michael Donovan. They both entered not guilty pleas. The jury

at the trial had to be heavily vetted to make sure none of them
had any connections to the police, Kirklees Social Services, or
the volunteers who had searched for Shannon. Shannon was
not called as a witness in the trial. Her evidence was deemed to
be problematic because she was nine years-old, confused, and
had been sedated by Karen Matthews (and Donovan) for
nearly two years. Shannon was deemed to be in no fit state to
offer evidence.

A big factor in not submitting evidence by Shannon was that
Shannon appeared to be struggling to separate fact from
fantasy by the end of her time at Lidgate Gardens. Shannon
told the police that Donovan's relatives visited him while she
was at the flat. The police could establish no evidence for this
though (only the fingerprints of Donovan and Shannon were
found in the flat) and it seemed somewhat unlikely that
Donovan would have had guests over while he was secretly
sheltering Shannon.

If the relatives were co-conspirators in the hoax (and it was of
course Donovan's relatives who were implicated in the
enduring whispers and conspiracies that surround this case)
why on earth would they visit Lidgate Gardens and risk being
seen by Shannon? That wouldn't make any sense. It is possible
that they were not involved and merely visited but the lack of
fingerprints suggested otherwise and would Donovan really
have answered his door to anyone - even relatives - with
Shannon hidden in the flat? The police felt that Shannon was
probably mistaken on this and so it was possible she was
mistaken on other things.

The tactics of the legal teams of Donovan and Karen Matthews
were simple. Donovoan's QC wanted everyone to think it was
all the fault of Karen Matthews. Karen's QC wanted everyone
to think it was all the fault of Michael Donovan. The real truth
was somewhere in the middle. They were both to blame. It was
clearly Karen Matthews who came up with the plan in the first
place. She was the dominant personality in the hoax. Michael
Donovan was however the main accomplice. Without him the

abduction could not have gone ahead and for this reason he had to take an equal share of the blame.

The police view of Michael Donovan and Karen Matthews was they were both world class liars and would essentially lie one another into submission in court. In the end they lied themselves into submission. It is fair to say that Donovan's evidence was more consistent and believable than that of Karen Matthews but it still had enough outlandish details to torpedo his credibility. It had already been established that Donovan was part of the abduction so his guilt was never really in question. In a sense what he said didn't strictly matter in terms of his own guilt but it did have consequences for Karen Matthews. She was already doomed but Donovan's evidence supplied a few extra nails to hammer into her legal coffin.

A Freedom of Information request to the Legal Aid Agency later found that Karen Matthews received £113,684 in crown court costs and Michael Donovan £114,310. Her pre-trial costs were £1,184 and Donovan's £2,944. These figures would obviously have been lower had they pled guilty. Donovan and Karen Matthews cost the taxpayer £250,000 for their trial. Karen Matthews and Michael Donovan had already cost the British taxpayer over three million pounds because of the massive one month police operation to look for Shannon. This had all turned out to be a very expensive hoax.

Karen Matthews and Michael Donovan were seated quite close together but they never once glanced at one another. A security officer was positioned between them just in case they got angry with one another. Donovan, in a navy blue top, sat slumped forward with hunched shoulders and stared vacantly ahead for most of the trial. He was given a special court assistant for the trial who sat next to him and explained what was happening. Karen Matthews, by contrast, often sat back with her arms folded. She was sulky and impatient throughout the trial and acted like someone who had been dragged here by mistake and was missing her favourite television show as a consequence. Karen Matthews still didn't quite seem to grasp how much trouble she was in. Karen's hair was tied up and she looked smart in a cream top.

The prosecution described Karen Matthews as a 'Jekyll and Hyde' character. They said she had two distinct personas during the search for Shannon which she alternated according to the situation. There was the public Karen Matthews who dealt with the media. The public version of Karen Matthews was a mumbly teary eyed mother who was lost in a nightmare of sorrow and could barely speak. Then there was the private Karen Matthews. The private Karen Matthews drank beer and cracked jokes. The private Karen Matthews didn't give two hoots that her daughter was missing because she knew only too well that her daughter wasn't really missing. The prosecution noted that some of Karen's friends and various police officers had seen the private version of Karen Matthews during the search for Shannon and been baffled by her strange behaviour.

Michael Donovan told the court that Shannon said he was much nicer than her parents. Donovan then portrayed himself in a positive light by saying that he'd purchased toys and games for Shannon out of his own money and took her for long drives so that she didn't get cabin fever and didn't feel trapped in the flat. Donovan even claimed that when he went to the supermarket he took Shannon and left her in the car. It seemed rather unlikely though that Shannon Matthews - at the time the most famous nine year-old in England - could have been left in a busy supermarket car park while Michael Donovan stocked up on frozen pizzas and Pokeman toys.

The tabloids made it sound like Shannon was a guest of Jeffrey Dahmer for a month while Michael Donovan made it sound as if Shannon had enjoyed a week at Butlin's. None of these general impressions were true at all. Donovan had been reasonably decent to Shannon but her captivity was definitely weird and definitely not something she enjoyed or wanted to experience for very long. Alan Conrad QC, who defended

Donovan, said in court of his client - "He is not an evil monster but a pathetic inadequate who was vulnerable, unsophisticated and weak in body and mind." Conrad also insisted that Donovan had been kind to Shannon. "She was treated by the defendant with a degree of respect and allowed her own space," he said.

Michael Donovan said he'd wanted no part of this abduction scam but Karen Matthews kept threatening him. When he was asked about the list of instructions for Shannon found on notes in his flat Donovan said they were nothing to do with him and that Karen Matthews had written them. Donovan's replies in court were short and to the point. He never really displayed much emotion. He had an advantage over Karen Matthews in that he stuck to one story all through his arrest to the trial. That at least made his evidence (whether truthful or not) easier to remember. Karen Matthews had a more complex task because she'd told so many different variations on her side of the story since her arrest that she must have been hopelessly confused herself by now. Donovan said the abduction plan had been cooked up in a Dewsbury cafe between him and Karen Matthews.

Frances Oldham QC had a simple defence plan for Karen Matthews. Oldham simply insisted that the abduction was cooked up by Donovan with his sister Alice Meehan and niece Amanda Hyett and that poor innocent Karen Matthews had nothing to do with at all. It was a preposterous claim. Of course Karen Mathews knew of the abduction. How could she not? One could feel some sympathy for Oldham from a professional point of view because she was trying to defend a compulsive liar who had told several different versions of what happened in police custody. Oldham faced an impossible task in court. Rumpole of the Bailey couldn't have got Karen Matthews a not guilty verdict. No one could.

On day twelve of the trial Karen Matthews was called to give evidence. She would spend two days being questioned in court and did not perform very well - though of course her case was hopeless to begin with. In response to questions by Frances Oldham QC, Karen insisted that she had nothing to do with the abduction plot and was not interested in any reward money. She also refuted the allegations of Michael Donovan that she had threatened him into going along with the abduction. Karen told the court she had no idea that Shannon was with Donovan at Lidgate gardens until she saw a news report saying that was where Shannon had been found. When she was asked why she hadn't shown much emotion when she was told that Shannon had been found, Karen said this was because she was initially overwhelmed by the news and felt as if she was in shock. She said the happiness and relief came later.

The court also heard about the evidence pertaining to others alleged to have played a role in the abduction. A delivery man named Mark Goode claimed he had delivered a bed to the house of Craig Meehan's mother when Shannon was found and distinctly heard someone on a telephone say - "Don't say nowt, just keep your mouth shut! They'll never, ever find out!" The court heard from a police officer who said that in one of her early interviews, after Shannon was found, Karen Matthews had said - "I don't know what I'm saying. The one involved is Amanda Hyett (Craig Meehan's sister). I told her everything and she said to keep it hush-hush, to think of the money we could make for holidays and things."

Caroline Meehan was called to give evidence and asked if she had been on the phone during the conversation the delivery driver supposedly heard. She could hardly deny this as telephone records indicated that she was indeed on the phone to her mother at the time the delivery man stipulated. Caroline Meehan said that the quotes attributed to her mother were never said on the phone and that she had absolutely nothing to keep quiet about. Caroline Meehan said she had no idea why she was being dragged into this sorry mess and knew nothing about the abduction. She said she was unaware of anyone else being involved in the hoax. In the end no charges were ever issued against Alice Meehan, Caroline Meehan, or Amanda

Hyett. There simply wasn't sufficient evidence to build a case.

The problem with Karen Matthews' defence was not just that it changed several times in custody (the court were naturally told about this) but also that it never made any sense. If she was planning to leave Craig Meehan why was Shannon, a nervous and meek nine year-old girl, sent on to Lidgate Gardens alone? Karen's claim that she had no idea where Donovan lived was destroyed when one of his neighbours identified her to police. Karen's claim that Craig Meehan was the real puppetmaster of the abduction hoax was also easily disproven. The police never found any evidence at all that Craig Meehan knew anything about the hoax.

Craig Meehan showed much more emotion than Karen when Shannon was found. The police said he seemed genuinely relieved. This was strange behaviour for someone who had supposedly arranged to have her kidnapped! Michael Donovan's claim that Karen had come up with the plan and he was weak and stupid enough to go along with it was much more believable to the police than the various scattershot conspiracy theories offered by Karen Matthews in police interview rooms and the court in Leeds.

The trial concluded at the start of December. A unanimous verdict was delivered by the jury on the 4th of that month. It had taken the jury only six hours to come to their conclusion. Karen Matthews and Michael Donovan were both eventually sentenced to eight years in prison. There was no reaction from the public gallery because the judge had warned that he didn't want any 'emotional' reaction to the verdict. What he obviously meant was that he didn't want anyone to start cheering. Karen stared straight ahead when the verdict was read. Her red hair was shoulder length and she'd worn the same cream jacket for the whole trial.

Michael Donovan was released from prison in April 2012. He was released a few weeks before Karen Matthews. How that must have infuriated Karen when she heard the news. All that mud she had slung in the direction of Michael Donovan for the last four years and he STILL got out before she did. The problem for Karen was that no one believed anything she said anymore. The police and prosecution were satisfied that Karen Matthews was the originator of the hoax and so it stood to reason that she would end up with a sentence which was at the very least comparable with that of Michael Donovan. She only had herself to blame.

Michael Donovan has rarely featured in the media since 2012. A few months after his release he was pictured in the tabloids vacantly sitting on a bench outside a cafe. The tabloids said that his parole officer had to come and pick him because he was creeping people out. Donovan was in Leeds at the time so clearly hadn't been moved very far - if at all. Donovan had another stint in prison later for fighting (which didn't sound much like the usually meek Donovan) but news about him is almost non existent now. Donovan has largely been left alone since 2012 by the media but that most definitely wouldn't be the case with Karen Matthews.

Those in prison with Karen Matthews in her last months behind bars say that was lost in delusions. Karen seemed to think she was now famous and would be a Jade Goody style celebrity on the outside world. More than one prisoner said that Karen told them she was going to appear on the Jeremy Kyle show after her release. Karen was released from Foston Hall prison in Derbyshire in April 2012. She had served less than four years of her eight year sentence. She was placed on licence for the remainder of her sentence and banned from ever returning to Dewsbury. Karen Matthews was definitely not the most popular person in Dewsbury. Many people there were still very angry at the deception Karen had engineered.

Karen Matthews ended up in a seaside town on the south coast which the tabloids said was known as Monsters By the Sea because the authorities had a habit of housing notorious criminals there when they got out of prison. Ian Huntley's former girlfriend Maxine Carr was alleged to have lived here too for a time when she got out of prison. The media are naturally not allowed to name this town. Karen was given a new identity on the outside but this was pretty pointless because she was still a very recognisable person. It's not as if she had plastic surgery or anything. Karen now went by the name of Kate in a rather futile attempt to hide who she really was. After she was discovered at Lidgate Gardens, Shannon eventually passed from being under police protection to the care of Kirklees Family Services. The media were gagged when it came to reporting on Shannon. She was given a new name and a new home. Shannon's contact with her siblings and father remained though and must have been a comfort to her.

A missing child hoax of the type that Karen Matthews and Michael Donovan attempted is surprisingly rare. Research in this area throws up hardly anything like the Shannon Matthews case. There have been cases where a mother has reported a missing child and it turned out the woman didn't even have a child in the first place. There have been cases where a hoaxer has posed as a grown up long lost child. Believe it or not there have even been cases where very young teenagers have hoaxed their own disappearance or abduction purely so they could spend time with a secret boyfriend. These days, online scams involving fictitious missing children are pretty common. What happened with Shannon Matthews though was exceptionally rare and almost in a league of its own.

This is as good an explanation as any for why the Shannon Matthews case still fascinates today. The Shannon Matthews case was like a black comedy written by a thriller writer. The fact that it was true made it all the more astonishing. The story even had a red herring and incredible twist when it was revealed that Michael Donovan wasn't even the main villain in this true crime case file! There was even a large dose of dark farce in this crime yarn. Karen Matthews and Michael Donovan always seemed comically unaware that they had about as much chance of collecting any reward money as Eddie Edwards did of winning a ski jump gold medal.

The blundering attempts of Karen Matthews and Michael Donovan to defend themselves were not without black humour either. We had Karen telling the police that she had no idea who Michael Donovan was or waving a teddy bear around at press conferences in a desperate attempt to impersonate Kate McCann. Not to be outdone, there was the ridiculous moment where Michael Donovan pretended to be surprised that an elastic tether had been found in his flat. Donovan might have well have gone the whole hog and attributed the tether to little pixies who came out at night to create mischief for the residents of Lidgate Gardens. This case though was no laughing matter. Karen's children, Shannon in particular, were the real victims. They all faced a tremendous upheaval to their young lives and although they almost certainly emerged with a better life as a consequence this was not a pleasant ordeal for any child to have to go through.

It was announced in September 2020 that Shannon Matthews and her siblings had been granted lifelong anonymity by the High Court. Shannon was about to turn 22. By now she and her siblings had all legally changed their names. The High Court issued a sweeping new order which meant that their new names, addresses and jobs could never be revealed or published unless a court overrules the decision or the family revoke it. This ended any lingering speculation about Shannon doing an interview or writing a book. She had decided to live her life out of the public eye. Shannon was clearly happy with the arrangements as they were and saw no reason to change anything.

LONDON'S MOST NOTORIOUS CANNIBAL

Dr Eric Hickey, professor of forensic psychology at Walden University, estimated that around only around five to ten out of every two thousand serial killers are cannibals. It is very rare for serial killers to eat the flesh of their victims. This fact makes the known cannibal serial killers all the more infamous. There are not a huge amount of killers where we know for a fact that they ate parts of their victims and so verified killers who fall into this category are (unavoidably) all the more macabre and morbidly fascinating. The most famous cannibal killer is of course the American serial killer Jeffrey Dahmer. Dahmer was convicted on 15 counts of first-degree murder. Dahmer fried the body parts of his victims in a skillet before he ate them. He used a meat tenderizer to make human flesh more tender and edible.

During his police confession, Jeffrey Dahmer was asked if he ate human body parts plain. He replied that he ate them with salt & pepper and steak sauce. Dahmer had a special tray at the bottom of his fridge to collect the blood that dripped down from body parts. Jeffrey Dahmer would sometimes make sandwiches for neighbours in his apartment building. It is therefore highly possible that his neighbours might have unwittingly eaten human flesh. Dahmer had a very (what else?) deadpan sense of humour. He would tell journalists in prison that human biceps tasted like a good cut of steak. Dahmer tends to be known as The Milwaukee Cannibal in true crime circles today. Dahmer said he ate parts of his victims because he wanted them to always be a part of him.

There have been cannibal killers in most nations around the world. Though rare, cannibal killers are not confined to any one country. Özgür Dengiz was a Turkish killer who killed two people and attempted to kill another. His crimes took place from 1997 to 2007. When he was captured, Dengiz was found to have human flesh in his fridge. Dengiz said he liked human flesh so much he would even eat it raw. Zhang Yongming was a Chinese serial killer responsible for at least eleven murders from 2008 to 2012. He sold the flesh of his victims at a local market and pretended it was ostrich meat. When he was arrested, the police found that Yongming had preserved human eyeballs in jars. The flesh of his victims was hanging up to dry. Alexander Bychkov was a Russian serial killer who killed nine men from 2009 to 2012. In his confession to the police, Bychkov claimed that he ate livers, hearts and the muscle of his victims.

Joachim Kroll was born in Hindenburg, Upper Silesia, in 1933. Kroll killed fourteen people between 1955 and 1976. When the police entered the apartment where Kroll lived there was a hand boiling in a pan of water and human flesh in the fridge. Human waste blocked the pipes and toilet. Kroll was clearly insane. He tends to be known as The Ruhr Cannibal in true crime articles. When he was asked to explain why he had eaten parts of his victims, Kroll calmly replied that he had done this to reduce his supermarket shopping bills for food. Dorángel Vargas was known as The Hannibal Lecter of the Andes. He killed at least fourteen people in the mid 1990s in Venezuela. Vargas was homeless and preyed on victims in a local park. He confessed to eating eleven of his victims. Vargas said he did not eat women or children because they were too pure. He also declined to eat overweight people because he said fatty flesh was less healthy.

Tamara Samsonova was born in 1947 in the city of Uzhur. Samsonova tends to be known as The Granny Ripper in true crime circles for reasons that will soon become clear. As a young woman she got married and worked for a travel agency. However her husband mysteriously vanished in 2000. Given what we now know about Tamara Samsonova it doesn't seem like a tremendously outrageous notion to suggest that she might have killed him. Tamara Samsonova was arrested in 2015 after CCTV captured her struggling with various bags which were then found to contain human body parts. The body parts belonged to 79-year-old Valentina Ulanova - who Samsonova was supposed to be caring for.

Samsonova had poisoned the woman and then dismembered her body with a hacksaw. "I came home and put the whole pack of Phenazepamum - 50 pills - into her Olivier salad,' she told the police. 'She liked it very much. I woke up after 2am and she was lying on the floor. So I started cutting her to pieces. It was hard for me to carry her to the bathroom, she was fat and heavy. I did everything at the kitchen where she was lying." Samsonova was also captured in the footage with a saucepan which contained the head of her victim.

The motivation for the murder? Samsonova said she had got fed up with Valentina Ulanova because Valentina had a habit of not washing out the tea cups properly after she'd used them. When the police arrested the 66 year-old Tamara Samsonova they found she had written diaries which featured extensive details on eleven murders she had carried out over the years. It was true too that the local area had had incidences of finding bags of human remains. Samsonova had dumped the headless body of Valentina Ulanova in a street before her arrest.

It was then established that in 2003 Tamara Samsonova had murdered a 44 year-old tenant who was staying with her. His headless and limb free body was also dumped in a street. "I killed my tenant Volodya," she told the police, "cut him to pieces in the bathroom with a knife and put the pieces of his body in plastic bags and threw them away in the different parts of Frunzensky District." The police, on searching the home of Tamara Samsonova, found that she seemed to be obsessed with black magic. This was clearly a nutty and disturbed woman. The Russian media reported that Tamara Samsonova was also a cannibal who claimed to have removed and eaten the lungs of one of her victims.

Tamara Samsonova was sent to a psychiatric treatment hospital while the police began the complicated and difficult task of trying to establish just how many people she did or didn't kill. The answer to that question at this time is anyone's guess. We know that Tamara Samsonova killed at least three people but the true figure could be four times that if her diaries are to be believed.

As for British cannibal killers, the most notorious example (at least in modern times) is probably a man named Peter Bryan. Peter Bryan was a killer who murdered three people in England from 1993 to 2004. When he was captured by the police in 2004, Bryan was cooking parts of a victim's brain in a frying pan. "I ate his brains with butter," Bryan told the police. "It was really nice." Bryan was completely insane. He was sent to Broadmoor Hospital - where he later killed another inmate because he said he wanted to eat more human flesh. The frightening thing about Peter Bryan (and there were obviously MANY frightening things about this man) is that Bryan had the ability to make people think that he was completely rehabilitated and posed no threat. Friends of Bryan and staff who treated him didn't seem to detect any danger about him at all - which turned out to be a very big and tragic miscalculation. When it comes to serial killers this is sometimes called the Mask of Sanity.

Bryan was born in London in 1969. He was the youngest of seven children. He attended Shaftesbury Junior School in Forest Gate, before attending Trinity Secondary School in Canning Town. Bryan is believed to have left school when he was about fifteen. He had various casual jobs including a stint working on a clothes stall at a market. It is believed he also worked in a soup kitchen for a brief period. The warning signs about Bryan first became apparent when he was eighteen years-old and was involved in a fracas after trying to throw another resident in his London tower block out of a sixth floor window. Thankfully, Bryan was not successful in this and the resident managed to avoid what almost certainly would have been a fatal fall.

Though the police were called out for this incident they took no action against Bryan and he seemed to escape with not much more than a slap on the wrist and a warning to behave himself in the future and not attempt to throw any more neighbours out of his tower block. The victim who had narrowly avoided being throw from the sixth floor said the attack on him by Bryan was completely unprovoked. Hindsight is obviously a wonderful thing but from what later transpired it is obvious that the authorities should have kept a closer watch on Peter Bryan. He was plainly a dangerous and disturbed young man with the capacity to cause someone serious harm.

Peter Bryan committed his first murder in 1993 when he was 23 years-old. At this time Bryan had recently (and briefly) worked in clothes shop on the Kings Road but lost his job when he was caught stealing some clothes. Bryan had apparently become infatuated with Nisha Sheth - though this infatuation ultimately manifested itself in the most tragic way imaginable. Nisha was the twenty year-old daughter of the owners of the clothes shop that Bryan had worked in. Because he had lost his job, Bryan decided he would get revenge on the owners of the shop by killing Nisha. He struck the unsuspecting Nisha over the head with a claw hammer while she was speaking to someone on the telephone and she was dead in matter of minutes. The murder was especially distressing and shocking because Bryan killed Nisha in full view of her younger brother Bobby. Bobby was twelve years-old and knocked to the floor by Bryan before the murder took place.

Bryan was a powerful looking and intimidating man. In some of his photographs he looks a bit like the late British heavyweight boxer Gary Mason - only much more sullen. After the murder of Nisha Sheth, Bryan then jumped from a balcony in what was obviously a suicide attempt. He was said to be high on cannabis when he murdered poor Nisha and was patently still in a confused and addled stare. The suicide attempt was unsuccessful and Bryan was arrested when the police arrived on the scene. He confessed to the murder of Nisha Sheth and was found guilty of manslaughter on the grounds of diminished responsibility.

Peter Bryan's next port of call was Rampton maximum security psychiatric unit. Despite the severity of his crime though, Peter Bryan did not appear to strike those who cared for him as dangerous or insane. In time they seemed to come to the conclusion that Peter Bryan was somehow cured - or at the very least no longer an immediate danger. In fact, in 2001 he was transferred to the John Howard Centre from Rampton and was now in the care of a social worker and psychiatrist. The staff who had treated Bryan said he had now tamed his attitude and anger issues and had made tremendous progress. Bryan's transfer from Rampton was only after the result of a six month trial period - which he evidently passed with flying colours. The Mask of Sanity worn by Peter Bryan was still firmly in place.

In 2002, Bryan was moved to a hostel in north London where he now had relative freedom. There were even plans to secure him independent accommodation. It seems rather bizarre that a man who murdered a young woman with a claw hammer now (only nine years later) essentially had a foothold back in society and was barely a prisoner at all anymore. Those who had looked after Bryan during his incarceration seemed to believe that the demons which drove him to murder had been banished. In this assumption they were to be proved completely wrong - with tragic and disturbing consequences. The authorities were clearly paving the way for Peter Bryan to perhaps even be completely released. To all intents and purposes, Bryan was practically like a free person already.

At the start of 2004, Bryan was sent to an open psychiatric ward at Newham General Hospital after being caught 'blowing raspberries' on the stomach of a sixteen year-old girl. In February 2004, Bryan then killed for the second time when he murdered 43 year-old Brian Cherry. Cherry was actually a friend of Bryan - not that it did him much good. The murder happened a mere three hours after Bryan had been discharged from his medical unit at the hospital. The murder took place at Cherry's flat in Walthamstow, east London. A woman named Nicola Newman arrived at the flat and was told by a blood splattered Peter Bryan that Cherry was dead.

Brian Cherry had been struck in the head 24 times with a hammer. One of his arms had been cut off and a leg had been severed. His head was partially sawed off and Peter Bryan was cooking brain and flesh from the head on a stove with some butter. The flesh he was cooking was matted with Cherry's hair. This was literally the most disturbing and horrific crime scene anyone could imagine. It later transpired that the staff supposed to be looking after Bryan had reduced the dosage of the medication he was taking after he complained. This was obviously not a terribly sensible thing to do and may have contributed to his tragic 'lapse'.

Peter Bryan was sent to Belmarsh Prison after the murder of Brian Cherry. He proved to be a volatile and unpredictable prisoner. He punched a prison officer and even constructed a noose in his cell in what was presumably a thought to suicide (though it could be that the noose was intended for another prisoner). In the end Bryan was sent to Broadmoor. Amazingly though, he was then transferred to a medium risk area. Believe it or not, despite hacking his friend to pieces and eating part of his brain, the authorities still didn't quite seem to understand how dangerous Bryan was! In April, 2004, Bryan killed a fellow inmate named Richard Loudwell.

The 59 year-old Loudwell was killed in the dining room. He had been strangled with a trouser cord and had his head smashed against the floor. The attack lasted for several minutes until the staff were alerted to the commotion and intervened. Bryan said he would have eaten Loudwell's brain if he hadn't been interrupted. Peter Bryan believed that killing and eating people made him stronger. He said he wanted to kill eight people so he could be a famous serial killer.

Bryan, who was suffering from paranoid schizophrenia, was so detached from reality that he still thought he was going to be released. On the 15th of March 2005, Bryan pleaded guilty at the Old Bailey to two manslaughters on the grounds of diminished responsibility. The tragic case of Peter Bryan led to much criticism of the way he had been given enough freedom to murder Brian Cherry. Social workers and care authorities simply hadn't kept a close enough watch on him. There were even criticisms from politicians - who understandably thought it was outrageous that a convicted murderer had basically been left to his own devices to go and kill again. Thankfully, Peter

Bryan is now highly unlikely to ever be given any degree of freedom again. Bryan is, for obvious reasons, sometimes called The Real Hannibal Lecter in true crime circles.

There aren't really that many examples of British cannibal killers besides Peter Bryan. You could probably say that Thomas Jefferies (was born in Dorset) counts. He was a violent criminal and rapist who was transported to Australia in 1823. Jefferies ended up in Van Diemen's Land (now Tasmania) and became a bushranger. Bushranger was the term used for escaped English convicts who roamed the outback of Australia getting up to all sorts of nefarious deeds as they tried to survive and evade capture. On arrival in Australia, Jefferies became the flagellator at Launceston Gaol. What this basically meant was that he was the chief flogger! Prisons were obviously a lot tougher in those days.

In 1825, Jefferies got into trouble for consorting with a female prisoner and also imprisoning a woman. On New Year's Eve he managed to escape with three other convicts. The convicts found a house several miles away in which a man named Mr Tibbs lived with his family. Jefferies and the convicts tied up Mr Tibbs, his wife, young child, and a neighbour who was at the house. The neighbour tried to fight back so the convicts shot him. Mr Tibbs was also injured in the fracas.

Jefferies and the convicts then left on foot with Mrs Tibbs and the baby. They wanted them as prisoners - or worse. Jefferies became frustrated when Mrs Tibbs lagged behind so he killed her baby. Mrs Tibbs was also raped. Somehow she managed to get away in the end and went home. She was understandably distraught and shaken by her horrific ordeal but she managed to supply the police with a description of Thomas Jefferies. Jefferies and the convicts eventually ran out of food and came to the brink of starvation. Their solution to this problem was grisly to say the least. They simply killed the weakest convict (a man named Russell) and ate some of him. Jefferies later said that he made some nice steaks from Russell.

In the middle of January 1826, Jefferies shot a constable dead and then joined a criminal gang. However, it appears that the criminal gang had no love for Thomas Jefferies and eventually turned him in to the authorities by revealing his location. Jefferies was captured before the end of January. However, as bargaining leverage, Jefferies then offered to tell the authorities all he knew about the identities and locations of wanted bushrangers. The gang that had turned Jefferies in (who were bushrangers themselves) were furious about this and already wishing they hadn't shopped him. They even considered a raid on the jail to kill him. Thomas Jefferies was hanged on the 4th of May 1826 at the old Hobart Jail. The information he divulged had led to the capture of some dangerous criminals but it hardly made up for the awful and horrific crimes he had committed in his own life.

Robert Maudsley is often referred to as a British cannibal killer but it is highly debatable if this is actually true. Robert Maudsley was born in Liverpool in 1953. Maudsley was not strictly a serial killer in the classic sense. He was capable of murder though and is regarded to be one of the most dangerous people ever to inhabit the British prison system. Maudsley's early years were dire by any standards. He grew up in an orphanage, was abused by his parents when reunited, and then came under the care of social services.

Maudsley then moved to London where he supported himself by becoming a rent boy. In 1974, a man picked up Maudsley for sex but then made a mistake by telling Maudsley he had abused children in the past. Maudsley was outraged by this and strangled the man. There was no trial as Maudsley was deemed insane and sent to Broadmoor. In 1977, Maudsley killed a a convicted paedophile at Broadmoor after torturing the man for nine hours in his cell. This was a very violent murder.

After this Maudsley was sent to Wakefield Prison. In 1978, Maudsley killed two more prisoners. The first was sex offender Salney Darwood - who was garrotted and stabbed. The second victim was Bill Roberts. Maudsley had fashioned a makeshift blade with a spoon for his murders. He jammed the weapon into the victim's ear. It was probably no great surprise that Robert Maudsley was isolated from other prisoners after this. He was simply too dangerous. Robert Maudsley had to be put in solitary confinement and have a special cell built. No one wanted to get too close to him. He is watched by several guards at all times.

Despite the brutality of his murders, Maudsley is said to have a high IQ and likes classical music. He has complained about the constrictive nature of his arrangements in prison but you might say that it was all his own fault. If he hadn't kept killing other prisoners he'd have been treated in a more normal fashion! Maudsley is often written of as a cannibal in true crime articles because it is claimed that he ate some of the brain of one of his prison victims after smashing his head in. This is probably an urban myth. Maudsley did not eat any of his victims. Of his crimes, Maudsley said - "When I kill, I think I have my parents in mind. If I had killed my parents in 1970, none of these people need have died. If I had killed them, then I would be walking around as a free man without a care in the world."

Cases like that of Peter Bryan where dangerous people are released or given relative freedom by the authorities only to murder again have happened many times. Britain's record on this front is better than most countries but there have still been some tragic cases. One such was that of Theodore Johnson. Theodore Johnson was born in Jamaica in 1954. In 1980 he moved to England with his wife Yvonne and worked in a garage. The couple lived in Wolverhampton. In 1981 the couple got into a violent argument as they were about to go to church. An altercation ensued and Johnson hit his wife over the head with a vase. He then pushed Yvonne to her death from the balcony of their ninth floor flat.

Surprisingly, Theodore Johnson was only convicted of manslaughter. The judge at the trial raised a few eyebrows for saying that Johnson had been provoked because his wife had a temper and was always nagging him. The judge didn't put it in those precise terms but that's more or less what he was trying to say. Theodore Johnson spent eleven years in prison and went back to Wolverhampton upon his release. He then began a relationship with a woman named Yvonne Bennett. The couple moved to London and had a child together. However, things turned sour because Yvonne Bennett started having an affair with another man. Theodore Johnson did not take this very well at all and began following Yvonne Bennett around and harassing her. In 1993 he strangled Yvonne Bennett to death using a belt.

At the Old Bailey trial, Theodore Johnson plead guilty to manslaughter on the grounds of diminished responsibility. He was sent to a secure mental hospital. Now, you might think that was the end of Theodore Johnson's sad story. He was a double killer in a secure mental institution. Case closed. Sadly though, there was a tragic coda yet to come. In 1994, Johnson was permitted to have some escorted parole and later do a City and Guilds course. During this time he met a woman named Angela Best. In 1997, Theodore Johnson was released by a mental health tribunal and told that he was not allowed to have a relationship with a woman unless he notified the authorities. Well, guess what? Johnson didn't tell the authorities about Angela Best and kept her a secret.

The couple had a long relationship but Best then decided to end it when she found out about Johnson's past convictions. In December 2016, Angela Best went to visit Theodore Johnson one last time to help him with some documentation he needed for a visit to the Jamaican Embassy. Theodore Johnson struck her several times with a hammer and then strangled her to death with a dressing gown cord. He then threw himself in front of a train at Cheshunt railway station. He survived but lost an arm and hand as a result of throwing himself in front of the moving train. Theodore Johnson was sentenced to 26 years in prison for the murder of Angela Best. He was now a triple killer (though strangely with only two convictions). The sentence, after an appeal, was later increased to 30 years. Hindsight is a wonderful thing but it seems reasonable to suggest that Theodore Johnson should never have been released unsupervised in the first place - let alone twice.

THE CASE OF THE DIAMOND PATTERNED WHIP

Neville Heath was born in Essex in 1917. Heath had a fairly normal background and eventually joined the RAF as a young man. However, his hoped for glittering military career was constantly gridlocked and interrupted by the fact that Heath was a petty criminal and completely unreliable. He'd frequently fail to show up for duty and was involved in all manner of dodgy sidelines - including theft and forgery. These crimes eventually earned him a stint in a borstal and spells in various cells. They were certainly the least of his crimes though. Heath was one of the most depraved killers in British criminal history - though his fame never really matched that of other killers of the era like John Christie and John Haigh. They say that truth is stranger than fiction and that is definitely the case with the life of Neville Heath.

Heath came from a fairly lower middle class background. His father was a barber and Heath went to a grammar school (gratuitous trivia - Heath went to the same school as future prime minister John Major). It is said though that Heath was dismayed to find that most of the other pupils at his school had much wealthier parents than he did and this made him enduringly obsessed with wealth and status. You could say that Neville Heath was a bit of a snob. He hated to be thought of as an ordinary person with no money. As a kid he was known to shoplift - although this was put down to lingering emotional scars caused by the tragic death of a brother.

Most experts think the theory that serial killers are 'bad seeds' who were born bad is a myth. You can't be born bad. Environments and experiences turn people twisted and bad - not genetics. A large number of serial killers had unhappy childhoods. There are exceptions to this of course but many serial killers had an awful start in life. In many cases they experienced grim poverty or suffered abuse - or in many cases experienced both of these factors. Neville Heath was definitely what you might describe as an exception to this rule. There didn't seem to be anything in his upbringing that would mark him out as a future killer of the most evil kind.

Many killers have convictions for sexual assault before they become murders. This wasn't the case with Neville Heath but there was an incident when he was about fifteen of Heath and some other boys attempting to sexually assault a girl. It is said that the girl's father (thankfully) intervened - whereupon Heath managed to talk his way out of trouble by saying it was all a prank which had got out of hand. Heath was a very persuasive talker. It is said that when he was at school the other pupils considered Heath to be a bad egg who they wouldn't trust as far as they could throw him. Despite this though they couldn't help but like him. Heath was cheeky and brash. He made them laugh with his antics and ingenious scams.

After he failed his exams at school, Heath had to get a job in a textile factory. He absolutely hated this job and resented having to do it. The world of nine to five and hum-drum reality definitely wasn't for Neville Heath. Heath decided that the people who always seemed to be respected the most in society were those in military uniform - especially if they had a rank and medals. Heath's daydreams were of becoming a military officer himself. He felt if he could do this then life would be a breeze. He could romance beautiful women and go to swanky parties. That tedious textile factory would then become a distant memory.

Heath now set his sights on joining the military and escaping from the tedious world of factory work. This led to him joining the RAF but he wrecked that with his persistent petty crimes. When he first joined the military, Heath was soon creating a fictitious autobiography for himself in an attempt to climb up the ladder. He would pretend he went to Eton or Oxford but in reality was a petty thief who flunked his way out of grammar school. He was kicked out of the air force in 1937 and spent some time in Nottingham pretending to be a young aristocrat. This ruse was rumbled when Heath tried to buy a car he had no money to pay for. He then got into trouble with the police for pawning stolen jewellery.

War was looming though and all branches of the armed services need fit young men. So, after being kicked out of the RAF, Heath joined the Royal Army Service Corps. The Royal Army Service Corps was the unit which was responsible for supplying the RAF with food, ammunition, and spare parts. It didn't have the prestige of being in the RAF but it was still a lot better than working in a factory. Heath was a fairly handsome and suave man with blond hair and blue eyes (in some of his photographs he looks rather like a young version of the actor Joss Ackland) who was good at coming up with fake identities and creating a fictitious character for himself to inhabit.

Heath was basically a highly accomplished con artist and one of the most convincing liars in criminal history. This was bad news for the poor women who were fooled by him. Because of his confidence and charm he also became something of a ladykiller - quite literally in this case. Heath was not just a smooth and debonair con artist but also a sexual sadist and murderer. And yet if you met Heath you wouldn't detect any danger from him. He didn't look like a killer and he was witty and charming. Many serial killers have a superficial sort of charm that serves as a mask to their real character. Heath had more charm than most killers though. He probably would have been entertaining company to have a drink with.

Heath had what you might describe as a colourful and eventful time in World War 2. He served in the Middle East but was court-martialed for going AWOL and also using a second pay-book to extract two sets of wages (that was a VERY Neville Heath sort of scam). He then absconded to South Africa and joined the air force there. While he was in South Africa, Heath sometimes used the fake name of Captain Selway. He mostly pretended though to be James Cadogan Armstrong - a fictitious South African born English aristocrat. Heath had a very vivid and fertile imagination. He would have made a good mystery writer. Heath also plainly had tremendous acting abilities and self-confidence. When you add this to his ruthless ambition then you can see how he made a very accomplished and dangerous criminal indeed.

In the end Neville Heath earned a court martial in South Africa for wearing medals that he hadn't won in combat. Neville Heath was plainly a man obsessed with the art of deception and appearances. Not to say that he wasn't capable of bravery though. Near the end of the war he joined the RAF again (presumably his past infractions were glossed over because the services needed all the men they could muster after several years of war and losses in manpower) and was cited for his courage during a bombing mission over Holland where Heath stayed on a stricken plane to help free a navigator. Knowing him as we do, Heath was probably thinking about the medal he might win for such an act.

Heath was married with a son but his wife got a separation on the grounds of desertion. Her husband was never around and never provided much in the way of financial support. Neville Heath was definitely not father of the year material. He was literally the worst role model any child could have so maybe it was for the best that he had little to do with his son in the end. Heath got married in South Africa. His wife was a young South African named Elizabeth Rivers who came from (no surprise here) a wealthy family. Heath's son was named Robert Michael Cadogan Armstrong - which obviously meant that Rivers and the South African authorities swallowed Heath's fake James Cadogan Armstrong character hook, line, and sinker. In the end Rivers did rumble his deception but apparently forgave him. Not that it mattered. He deserted her anyway.

After the war Heath tried to go back to South Africa again but his wife wanted nothing to do with him anymore and he was eventually deported. Heath was said to be a heavy drinker by now and frittered away what little money he had in pubs. It could be that he went back to South Africa because he had run out of money and wanted to get back in his wife's good books because her family were loaded. By now though it was too late. Heath had blown the chance he had of a good life and marriage in South Africa. He ended up living with his parents in London for a time - which must have been rather humiliating for a man of Heath's ambition and snobbery.

Heath now decided to join the Royal Institute of Navigation and become a commercial pilot. He began a course but when his criminal background was discovered he was booted off the course and his dreams of becoming a pilot came to an abrupt end. With no career prospects, Heath now devoted his time to romancing and conning women. Most of his time was now spent in pubs and dance halls. When it came to his own deceptions, Neville Heath was naturally most interested in women who might have some money. He would add titles to his name to impress them. Heath would pretend he was an RAF Group Captain or an officer in the army.

These deceptions seemed to work as he always impressed the families of the women he met. Heath liked tweed suits and smoked a pipe. He looked more like a Tory MP than a serial killer. Heath used a battery of assumed names as he sought to romance and swindle his way to financial security. Heath's many aliases included A. J. Banham, James Bulman, Capt Blyth, Bruce Lockhart, Sqn Ldr Walker, Lieut Col Graham, and Lord Dudley.

The story of Neville Heath sounds very Dirty Rotten Scoundrels so far doesn't it? You could even say that he seems like a likeable enough bounder. Well, rest assured, the Neville Heath story now gets considerably darker. Neville Heath was not likeable in the least and his story was no laughing matter. Heath now took up with a young woman named Yvonne

Symonds - who he pretended was his wife (though she wasn't). By now, Heath was pretending to be a Lieutenant Colonel and took a room at a hotel in Notting Hill. He agreed to marry Yvonne Symonds and she went back to her family in Worthing, Sussex, to tell them this news. They must have been pretty impressed to learn that Yvonne was now engaged to an urbane army officer. Little did they know the real truth of the matter.

Despite telling Yvonne he wanted to marry her, this didn't stop Heath from pursuing other women though. Heath didn't just pursue women in the hope of fleecing money. He also pursued women to cater to much baser and more disturbing desires. During part of 1946, when Heath was staying at a hotel in Notting Hill Gate, he went out for some drinks and ended up dancing with a woman named Margery Gardner. They are believed to have first meet at the Panama Club in Kensington - a place where Heath evidently went on the prowl looking for women quite often. Bumping into Neville Heath was literally the worst thing in the world that could have happened to Margery. She had no idea how dangerous he was.

Heath invited Margery to have dinner with him one night and she agreed to do this. That would turn out to be a tragic mistake. Margery was 32 and a film extra and artist. She had a young daughter and was recently separated from her husband. Margery was vulnerable enough to fall for the smooth patter and lies of Neville Heath. About four days after Yvonne Symonds had departed for Sussex, Heath and Margery Gardner spent the night together at his hotel room in Notting Hill. The next afternoon, around two, a maid found she couldn't get into the room to change the towels and linen so she asked her father (who was the hotel manager) to open the door.

Margery Gardner was found dead inside the room by the shocked hotel staff. She was restrained and naked on the bed and had been severely whipped and then suffocated with a pillow. Her nipples were almost bitten off. It is believed that many of these injuries were inflicted while she was still alive.

She had seventeen whip marks, had been raped, and an object had been inserted inside of her. Margery Gardner was basically the victim of a sadistic maniac. That sadistic maniac was Neville Heath. Heath was, to use a cliche, was the ultimate wolf in sheep's clothing. Pathologist Keith Simpson found diamond shapes on Margery's body which suggested this pattern had been on the whip. The pathologist told the police they if they found the whip used on Margery Gardner then they would have the killer.

Meanwhile, Heath had taken a train to Worthing to see Yvonne Symonds - whom he had agreed to marry (whether he was actually serious about this is open to question - he probably just wanted whatever money her family might have). Given that Margery Gardner had been found dead in Heath's hotel room it was pretty obvious that the police were now going to want to talk to him. Heath was well aware of this. He had (stupidly in hindsight) checked into the hotel using his real name. This suggested that he hadn't intended to kill anyone there and that the murder of Margery Gardner was a crazy spur of the moment act where he just couldn't help himself. Heath was - to put it mildly - now in something of a pickle.

When he arrived in Sussex, Heath was well aware that the murder of Margery Gardner was all over the newspapers and that the police in London wanted to talk to him. Heath told Yvonne about the murder and tried to talk his way out of trouble. Heath seemed to imply to Yvonne that Margery was a prostitute - which definitely wasn't the case. Heath told Yvonne that he'd kindly lent to his room to a gentleman because the gentleman in question wanted to spend the night with Margery. Heath said that this gentleman must have then murdered her. That was a blatant lie. Neville Heath had murdered Margery.

Rather than turn himself in for questioning, Heath then wrote to the police and told them a similar fictitious story to the one he had told Yvonne. By now the police were demanding that

Heath give himself up and were appealing for any information the public might have concerning his whereabouts. They obviously didn't know that he was in Sussex. Heath's letter to the police was as follows...

Sir,

I feel it to be my duty to inform you of certain facts in connection with the death of Mrs Gardner at Notting Hill Gate. I booked in at the hotel last Sunday, but not with Mrs Gardner, whom I met for the first time during the week. I had drinks with her on Friday evening, and while I was with her she met an acquaintance with whom she was obliged to sleep. The reasons, as I understand them, were mainly financial. It was then that Mrs Gardner asked if she could use my hotel room until two o'clock and intimated that if I return after that, I might spend the remainder of the night with her. I gave her my keys and told her to leave the hotel door open. It must have been almost 3 a.m. when I returned to the hotel and found her in the condition of which you are aware. I realised that I was in an invidious position, and rather than notify the police, I packed my belongings and left. Since then I have been in several minds whether to come forward or not, but in view of the circumstances I have been afraid to. I can give you a description of the man. He was aged approx. 30, dark hair (black), with small moustache. Height about 5' 9" *slim build. His name was Jack and I gathered he was a friend of Mrs Gardner of some long standing. I have the instrument with which Mrs Gardner was beaten and am forwarding this to you to-day. You will find my fingerprints on it, but you should also find others as well.*

N. G. C. Heath

The letter was classic Neville Heath. He seemed to arrogantly believe that he could lie his way of trouble simply by sending the police a letter! Like most crazed killers he was completely detached from reality. When he mentioned the 'instrument' with which Margery was beaten, Heath was making reference

to the whip. However he did not, as promised, send this whip
to the police. What he did instead was take a train to
Bournemouth over eighty miles away and check into the
Tollard Royal Hotel. Heath checked into the hotel under the
name Group Captain Rupert Brooke.

While in Bournemouth, Heath met a 21 year-old woman
named Doreen Marshall on the promenade and the old
patented Neville Heath charm and lies were soon venturing
forth. Legend has it that Heath approached Doreen on the
beach when she stopped to watch a Punch and Judy show.
Dorren had actually read of the murder of Margery Gardner in
the newspaper but - alas - she hadn't seen a picture of the
suspect the police wanted to question. That suspect was of
course the unmistakable square-jawed Neville Heath. Doreen
was in Bournemouth for a short holiday after a bout of measles
and influenza. Her doctor had prescribed some sea air so she
ended up in Bournemouth. Though there was no way she
could have anticipated this, the choice of Bournemouth would
cost Doreen her young life.

Heath persuaded Doreen to dine with him that evening in the
lounge of the hotel he was staying at. After that evening ended,
Doreen vanished apparently without trace. The manager of the
hotel where Doreen was staying then reported her
disappearance to the police. He knew that she had dined at
another hotel before she vanished. This was obviously the
hotel where Heath (masquerading as Group Captain Rupert
Brooke) was staying. Heath had been seen dining with Doreen
so he was now deemed suspicious and told by the manager of
his own hotel that he ought to see the police and tell them
anything he knew.

It didn't help matters for Heath that his image was now on
wanted posters in London in connection to the death of
Margery Gardner. The manager of the hotel told the police
that Doreen seemed uncomfortable in the presence of the man
she was dining with. The last sighting of Doreen had been of
her getting into a taxi with Heath after dinner. The body of

Doreen Marshall was found on Branksome Dene Chine by a dog walker. Branksome Dene Chine is a long sandy beach in Poole. The dog walker had been alerted to the body because it was attracting a lot of flies.

Doreen's throat had been slashed and one of her nipples bitten off. The mutilation of the body was very severe and disturbing (a Y shape was carved into her torso) and there was ample evidence of sexual assault (Heath had rammed what appeared to be a tree branch inside of her). A redness on Doreen's collar-bones indicated that Heath had forcibly sat on her and she had at least one broken rib. Her hands were full of defensive stab wounds from where she had been frenziedly attacked with a knife. There was also plenty of evidence that poor Doreen had been beaten to the head in savage fashion. Heath had taken Doreen down to the beach after their dinner and raped and murdered her. He had then slunk back to his hotel and climbed back into his room using the outside of the building.

Heath now went to the police and told them he had last seen Doreen in Bournemouth Gardens. He was still arrogant enough to believe he could talk his way out of this with bluster and lies - not to mention his fake identity. Neville Heath was eventually doomed though by Doreen's parents. They had come down to join the search for her and bumped into 'Group Captain Rupert Brooke' in the police station. They were pretty sure he was the infamous Nevile Heath - wanted on suspicion of murder and plastered on the news.

The police detained Heath and when they searched his possessions they found some of Doreen's belongings and a diamond patterned whip. This was the whip that had been used on Margery Gardner. They also found Heath had a scarf with Margery's blood on it. It is believed that Heath had used this scarf to stop Margery Gardner from screaming when he raped and killed her. During the court trial there seemed to be a general suggestion that Margery Gardner liked bondage games and was initially happy to be tied up by Heath. What he did in the end though was definitely not consensual.

By now the penny had completely dropped. The police knew that Group Captain Rupert Brooke and Neville Heath were one and the same. This man had murdered Margery Gardner in London and Doreen Marshall in Bournemouth. The game was finally up for Neville Heath and he was taken to London to face the music. Upon his arrest, he is alleged to have told his solicitor - "Women? They're weak and stupid. Basically crooked. That's why they're always attracted to rascals like me. They have the morals of alley cats and minds like sewers. They respond to flattery like a duck responds to water. Put me down as 'not guilty', old boy."

Heath tried to plead insanity (though he was highly reluctant to do this because he feared being sent to Broadmoor) at his trial but doctors insisted he was perfectly sane and simply a sexual sadist and killer who knew exactly what he was doing when he killed those women. William Bixley, who worked at the Old Bailey and had seen many famous murderers in the dock, said there was something about Neville Heath which chilled him to the bone. It was the fact that Heath seemed SO ordinary that made his crimes disturbing. "Heath seemed ostensibly so normal, and one had deep forebodings that only by a hair's breadth did other seemingly decent and pleasant young men escape from the awful sexual sadism which, at times, makes man lower than any animal that walks or crawls on the face of the earth."

Heath's trial lasted for three days. There were large crowds because people wanted to catch a glimpse of this charming and depraved ladykiller of legend for themselves. Heath was pretty unflappable during the trial. There was never any point in custody where he seemed to be distressed or anguished. From prison, he wrote a letter to a friend in which he said 'I honestly don't give a damn what happens to me. I have faced death too often in the past six years to worry about it. Anyway, I've nothing to live for since I lost my wife and child.' Heath claimed his heavy drinking caused blackouts and that he had no memory of killing the two women he had murdered.

Neville Heath was hung on the 16th of October 1946 at Pentonville Prison. He was 29 years-old. Heath had a large whisky before he went to the gallows. A day later he had his own waxwork at at Madame Tussauds in London. The diamond-patterned riding crop that Heath had used on Margery Gardner was later put on display in a police museum. It transpired that another woman had previously been tied up by Heath in a hotel room but had a lucky escape when her screams alerted hotel staff. The woman in question was named Pauline Brees and the incident took place in February 1946 in the Strand Palace Hotel in London. Heath had seduced Brees and she then woke up bounded and gagged in a bed with Heath looming over her. When she screamed (as best she could given the circumstances) Heath knocked her out.

Thankfully, the hotel staff did hear the cries and intervened. The police were called over this case but Heath had a very lucky escape because Pauline Brees decided not to press charges. Maybe she was too embarrassed by the incident to go through with a court appearance. It is clear though that Brees had a very close shave with death. Heath would almost certainly have killed her if the hotel staff hadn't interrupted him. Heath is suspected of a third murder but so far this has proved impossible to verify. It seems highly plausible though that the victim tally of Neville Heath could be higher than the record books state.

The story of Neville Heath is like the plot of a horror thriller. Indeed, none other than Alfred Hitchcock planned to make a film loosely based on Heath's life and crimes in the 1960s but never got around to this. In a letter to Hitchcock concerning a proposed film on Heath, the screenwriter Benn Levy wrote - 'It's got to be (based on) Heath, not (John George) Haigh (the acid bath murderer). Told forwards, the Heath story is a gift from heaven. You'd start with a 'straight' romantic meeting, handsome young man, pretty girl. Maybe he rescues her from the wild molestations of a drunken escort. 'I can't stand men who paw every girl they meet.' Get us rooting for them both. He perhaps unhappily married and therefore a model of screen-hero restraint. She begins to find him irresistibly 'just a little boy who can't cope with life' -- least of all with domestic problems such as he has described. She's sexually maternal with him, she'd give him anything -- and we're delighted. Presently a few of us get tiny stirrings of disquiet at the physical love-scenes but don't quite know why. By the time we see the climax of his love in action and her murder, then even the slowest of us get it! But we shouldn't know till then.'

Neville Heath is sometimes compared to Gordon Frederick Cummins because they were similar sorts of killers (they both had an RAF connection too) and only a few years separated their crimes (so one could say that they were more or less from the same era). Gordon Frederick Cummins was a killer who became known as The Blackout Ripper for murdering four women during the German bombing raids on London in World War 2. Cummins, who was in the Royal Air Force, was a very sick and savage killer. He slashed one woman's throat with a can opener and would sexually mutilate the victims. His first victim was a prostitute named Mabel Church in 1941. She was found strangled on Hampstead Heath. Around four months later at the start of 1942 he murdered Evelyn Hamilton.

The body of Hamilton was found at an air raid shelter in Marleybone. A prostitute named Evelyn Oatley was also found dead around the same time. She was another victim of Cummins. Not long after this a prostitute named Margaret Florence Lowe was found dead in Marleybone. Her wounds were very gruesome. She had been mutilated with a razor blade and knife. A day later a prostitute Doris Jouannet was murdered in Bayswater by Cummins. She was throttled with a silk scarf and then mutilated in his usual fashion. Two days later, Cummins met a woman named Margaret Hayward in Piccadilly and had some drinks with her in a pub. He then followed her out of the pub when she left and started to strangle her in an alley. Cummins was disrupted by a delivery boy and fled the area but he left his RAF gas mask at the scene of the crime. Gordon Frederick Cummins, thankfully, was not the most careful killer when it came to evidence. His attacks were so frenzied that he barely seemed to think about any clues he might be leaving behind.

In one of his earlier murders the police had obtained Commins' fingerprints at the crime scene but - frustratingly - couldn't identify the attacker and get a match. Cummins last potential victim was Kathleen Mulcahy - a prostitute he met near Paddington Station. They went to her flat but when Cummins tried to strangle her she bravely fought him off and screamed with such ferocity that he simply gave her some money to stop screaming and fled. Cummins had though left his RAF belt in the flat. The Air Ministry were called in to identify the gas mask and belt and managed to confirm that they had been issued to a certain Gordon Frederick Cummins. The fingerprints of Cummins were - of course - then matched to those found at the murder scenes and Margaret Hayward later identified Cummins as the man who had attacked her.

Cummins was only convicted of the murder of Evelyn Oatley but that was more than sufficient to earn him the most severe sentence possible. Gordon Frederick Cummins was hanged in Wandsworth Prison on June the 25th 1942. Despite the grisly nature of his crimes and that fact that he was a highly dangerous and sadistic killer, Cummins isn't actually that well known today. This is because the authorities suppressed the news of the murders at the time. Given the circumstances the authorities decided that Londoners had more than enough to worry about being pounded by the Luftwaffe each night and felt that throwing a serial killer panic into the mix was the last thing anyone needed. The close proximity of the murders suggests that Cummins was pretty out of control and quite prolific. Heaven knows how many people he would have killed if he hadn't been so careless and got caught.

Neville Heath is also sometimes compared to Robert Hicks Murray. Robert Hicks Murray became famous for what was known as The Eastbourne Tragedy in 1912. Murray was a bigamist and had two wives. He also had children with each wife. Murray was essentially a fraudster and con artist. He made up all manner of untruths about his life and background. The true nature of his background is generally unknown. All we do know is that he was a compulsive liar. His wives were sisters named Florence and Edith Paler. How he managed to live these two secret lives beggars belief (you'd think two sisters would realise they were married to the same man wouldn't you?) but he apparently explained his time away from each wife by saying he was on duty with the army.

Tragedy struck when Murray (which wasn't even his real name) fell in love with a young girl. The only problem was that he had two families already. Murray realised it would be impossible to maintain two wives AND a third lover and came up with a deadly solution to his dilemma. Murray he told his wives they were going on holiday to Eastbourne and rented a house there. It wasn't a holiday Murray had in mind though but murder. He brought Edith and their one year-old daughter Winifred to Eastbourne first and killed them both with a revolver. Two days later he brought Florence and their two children to the house and killed them too - or so he believed. Florence actually somehow survived being shot in the neck.

Murray then set fire to the bodies in an attempt to burn them but Florence (who Murray was obviously unaware had survived) managed to call for help. By this stage it all become too much - even for a man as cold hearted as Murray. Realising the game was up, Murray shot himself with his own revolver. Scotland Yard later believed that Robert Hicks Murray was probably in reality a man named Robert Henry Money. Money was a businessman and builder who was once suspected of having an involvement in his sister's death. However, one of Robert Henry Money's brothers wasn't convinced by this theory and didn't believe Murray was his estranged brother.

The theory that Murray was really Robert Henry Money came

as a consequence of the fact that the recovering Florence was shown a picture of Money and identified him as her late husband. The police investigation into this case led them to believe that Robert Hicks Murray had probably killed several wives in the past. It seems plausible as he was a serial bigamist and a very ruthless man. This would - if true - take the victim tally of Robert Hicks Murray up to ten and make him one of the worst killers in British history. However, such is the fog of mystery that surrounds Robert Hicks Murray the real truth is almost impossible to verify.

An interesting piece of trivia is that Neville Heath was said to drink in some of the same London pubs as John Haigh so they most likely knew each other. One could say that they were cut from a similar cloth when it came to deception and crime - though their methods were different. John George Haigh was born in Lincolnshire in 1909. Haigh was a British serial killer known as The Acid Bath Murderer. He killed at least six people but (as ever with serial killers) the real body count might be higher. Haigh was basically a thief and conman who became inspired by the tale of Georges-Alexandre Sarret, a French killer who used sulphuric acid to dispose of victims. Haigh simply deduced that if he killed the people he had robbed and conned and dissolved their bodies in acid then no one would ever be able to finger him for any crimes.

In his younger years, Haigh worked as a chauffeur but pretended to be a solicitor. Like Neville Heath, he was a very urbane sort of character who was able to deceive people (who should have known better) and win their trust. He was involved in dealing bogus stock shares and a compulsive thief. He is believed to have spent some time in prison during these years. Haigh, upon release, ruminated on his life and came to a rather disturbing conclusion. He decided that the reason why his career in crime had not taken off in the fashion he wanted was that the people he had swindled had been able to report him to the police. Why not simply kill the people he swindled? That way there would be no one to report his crimes.

Inspired by macabre tales of the French killer Georges-Alexandre Sarret, Haigh set upon what he felt was a surefire way to cover his tracks and dispose of his victims. To test his dark theory, Haigh murdered a man and seized the man's bank savings and pension. He even sold the victim's house. The victim was William McSwan - a former employer of Haigh. Haigh was jealous of McSwan's luxury lifestyle and this was the motivation for the murder. He murdered McSwan by clubbing him over the head and dissolved the body in a vat of acid. When the parents of William McSwan became suspicious of their son's disappearance and asked Haigh about his whereabouts he killed them too in similar fashion.

Haigh was said to have run up large gambling debts around this time and, needing more money to fund his lifestyle, he decided to kill again. His targets this time were Dr Archibald Henderson and his wife Rose. Haigh stole a revolver from Henderson and used it to shoot both of them dead. Haigh then dissolved them in acid and sold all of their possessions. He did though keep their dog and car for himself.

There were six verified victims of Haigh in all but he is believed to have killed as many as nine people. He would move around a lot and often stay in hotels. When money became tight again he would simply look for some new wealthy victims to kill so that he could ransack their property and bank accounts. Haigh was very crafty and would often forge legal documents from his victims handing over their houses and finances to him. John George Haigh was undone because of his past convictions for theft and fraud. When the police decided to investigate him in relation to some recent crimes they found that Haigh now lived in rooms with no drain access. Haigh had dissolved his latest victim in acid but then covered it in rubble (rather than dispose of it down the drain). The rubble was rather suspicious and the police investigated and thus revealed the dark secret of John Haigh.

The police proved there was human fat and remains in the rubble and - as a consequence - Haigh was sentenced to death and hung in 1949. The police actually found part of a foot in the rubble. Before he was hung, Haigh confessed to a number of murders which could never be verified because there was (obviously, given his strategy of dissolving victims in acid) no actual evidence or remains. His other victims are alleged to include two women. Haigh, urbane to the end, asked for a large brandy before his execution. He was a very calculating and ruthless man who only seemed to be interested in money. If he had to kill someone to get his hands on money it didn't bother him in the least.

www.ingramcontent.com/pod-product-compliance
Lightning Source LLC
Chambersburg PA
CBHW031407150726

47989CB00002B/572